PRENTICE HALL
FOUNDATIONS OF MODERN SOCIOLOGY

Alex Inkeles, Editor

third edition

SOCIETY AND POPULATION

DAVID M. HEER
University of Southern California

JILL S. GRIGSBY
Pomona College

Prentice Hall, Englewood Cliffs, New Jersey 07632

Library of Congress Cataloging-in-Publication Data

Heer, David M.

　Society and population / David M. Heer and Jill S. Grigsby. —3rd ed.
　p. cm. —(Prentice Hall foundations of modern society series)
　Includes bibliographical references and index.
　ISBN 0-13-819707-5 (paper)
　1. Population. 2. Demography. I. Grigsby, Jill. II. Title. III. Series.
HB851.H4　1992
304.6—dc20　　　　　　　　　　　　　　　　　　　91-25782
　　　　　　　　　　　　　　　　　　　　　　　　　　　　CIP

Acquisitions Editor:　Nancy Roberts
Copy Editor:　Nancy Andreola
Prepress Buyer:　Kelly Behr
Manufacturing Buyer:　Mary Ann Gloriande

 ©1992, 1975, 1968 by Prentice-Hall, Inc.
A Simon & Schuster Company
Englewood Cliffs, New Jersey 07632

Printed in the United States of America
10　9　8　7　6　5　4　3　2　1

0-13-819707-5

Prentice-Hall International (UK) Limited, *London*
Prentice-Hall of Australia Pty. Limited, *Sydney*
Prentice-Hall Canada Inc., *Toronto*
Prentice-Hall Hispanoamericana, S.A., *Mexico*
Prentice-Hall of India Private Limited, *New Delhi*
Prentice-Hall of Japan, Inc., *Tokyo*
Simon & Schuster Asia Pte. Ltd., *Singapore*
Editora Prentice-Hall do Brasil, Ltda., *Rio de Janeiro*

CONTENTS

CHAPTER **9**

POPULATION AND POLITICAL POWER,   *87*

CHAPTER **10**

POPULATION LEGISLATION AND POLICY,   *93*

PREFACE

It is fitting that a series on modern sociology would include a volume on population, for the study of population (demography) can lead to a better understanding of social structure and social problems. This book emphasizes the fundamental, classic research findings of demography that have endured over time and continue to inform current population research.

Since the second edition was published in 1975, new demographic issues have emerged, which we have attempted to cover in this edition. For example, the environmental problems of global warming and nuclear disasters, practically unheard of in the early 1970s, have appeared regularly in the popular media in recent years. Acquired immune deficiency syndrome (AIDS) has altered the course of mortality trends across the world. Through data collection efforts like the World Fertility Survey and the European Fertility Project, our knowledge of child bearing patterns has extended both geographically and historically. International migration trends and policies have also undergone radical change. The 1970s and 1980s witnessed drastic fertility reduction policies in China; other societies wrestled with below-replacement fertility. The United States, like many other countries, has recast abortion policies as the political winds have shifted. These new topics have questioned and elaborated on earlier theoretical assumptions and empirical findings.

We would like to express our appreciation to all those who have helped in the preparation of earlier editions and of this third edition. We would like to thank Alex Inkeles, the general editor of the Prentice Hall Foundations of Modern Sociology Series, who made valuable suggestions that helped us to organize this work; James McKenna and Hans Palmer for their suggestions;

Laurel Smith for providing research assistance; and Gail Orozco, for preparing tables and furnishing word processing support. The National Institute on Aging, through the Ethel Percy Andrus Center at the University of Southern California, partially funded Jill Grigsby's work.

SOCIETY
AND
POPULATION

CHAPTER 1
THE GROWTH OF WORLD POPULATION

THE HISTORY OF HUMAN POPULATION GROWTH

Even today we do not know with certainty the actual size of populations in many parts of the world; thus it is not surprising that we can only estimate the number of persons living at each stage of human existence. Careful analyses of available data, however, point to one sure aspect of the expansion of human population: for 99 percent of human history, population growth was extremely small, while the most recent period has witnessed truly prodigious growth.[1]

In considering the history of human population growth, we must first decide what we mean by "human." Humans have descended from other primates, yet we have no clear picture of all the links between humans and their prehominid ancestors. Moreover, even if all the links were apparent, we would still have the problem of defining when "humans" themselves appeared. For instance, do we wish to define humans as beginning with the appearance of the family *Hominidae*, the genus *Homo*, or the species *Homo sapiens*? If we choose to trace the population history of the family *Hominidae*, we may have to go back 5 1/2 million years; if we confine our interest to *Homo sapiens*, we need go back only around 50,000 years.

Perhaps the most important stage in human evolution was the appearance of terrestrial, rather than tree-dwelling, creatures of fully upright posture who were able not only to use tools but also to make them. The family *Hominidae* comprises all such creatures. The first individuals to fit definitely into this category, who now bear the technical name *australopithecines*, developed during the geological epoch before ours (the Pleistocene) perhaps as long as 5 1/2 million years ago. Free to use their flexible hands to grasp objects for digging and collecting, the australopithecines foraged across the savannahs of Africa.[2] It is difficult to say exactly when it happened, but gradually, perhaps a couple of million years ago, these human ancestors become the first mammals to depend on tools and, thus, culture for survival.[3] The development of tools for gathering and eventually for hunting may have been responsible for longer survival and, relative to other primates, a shorter birth interval, which permitted population expansion at a moderate rate.[4]

For the earliest periods of human history, we have no direct counts, like censuses, to measure population size. Instead, anthropologists and historians estimate the number of persons who, given the way of life at a particular point in time, would have been able to subsist. One million years ago there were only 125,000 tool-using hominids (including *Homo erectus*), but by 8000 B.C. the population of *Homo sapiens*, by then the only hominid, was 5.3 million and growing.[5] Around 8000 B.C., with the onset of agriculture, the population began to increase more rapidly, reaching 300 million by A.D. 1, the time of the Roman census. By 1750 the population had grown to approximately 800 million, and at this point the extremely rapid population growth began, as Table 1–1 shows. Population growth continued to accelerate until the 1970s, when the rate of growth began to subside. Even during the 1980s, however, the population growth rate was still a large 17 per 1,000, enough for the world's population to double in just 41 years. Clearly, this last half-century has produced unprecedented rates of population growth in human history. While

Table 1–1. Estimated Population of the World since A.D. 1

YEAR	POPULATION	AVERAGE ANNUAL RATE OF INCREASE (PER 1,000)	AVERAGE ANNUAL NUMBERS ADDED (MILLIONS)
A.D. 1	300	--	--
1650	545	0.4	0.2
1750	728	3	1.8
1800	906	4	3.6
1850	1,171	5	5.3
1900	1,608	6	8.7
1950	2,515	9	18.1
1960	3,019	18	50.4
1970	3,698	20	67.9
1980	4,450	19	75.2
1990	5,292	17	84.2
2000	6,251	17	95.9
2010	7,191	14	94.0
2025	8,467	11	85.1

Source: The estimate of population size at A.D. 1 is from Coale, Ansley J. "The History of the Human Population"; *The Human Population* "A Scientific American Book" (San Francisco: W. H. Freeman and Company), 1974. Population and growth rate estimates from 1650 to 1900 are from Carr-Saunders, A. M; *World Population: Past Growth and Present Trends* (Oxford: Clarendon, 1936), p. 42. Population estimates from 1950 to 2025 are from United Nations, Department of International Economic and Social Affairs, *World Population Prospects 1988* (New York: United Nations, 1989), p. 28.

the rate of population growth has already begun to decline, the numbers added each year will continue to increase until some time after the year 2000, barring major catastrophes. Because both the absolute number added each year and the average growth rate have consequences for the human condition, the task of reducing population growth has not yet ended.[6]

It is important to note that the world population growth rates listed in Table 1–1 are averages, over both time and space. Within each time interval and among regions of the world lies great variation. Before the introduction of agriculture, hunting and gathering societies tended to grow very slowly, although migrations to new territories allowed for moderate population growth during limited time periods. Agricultural technologies brought extreme variations in population growth among the regions of the world. While some parts of the world suffered population losses through epidemics, wars, or bad weather conditions, other places could be experiencing population growth at the same time. Before 1000 A.D., for example, subpopulations of central and western Europe declined by as much as one-half, then started to grow again. China's population size also fluctuated in size during this period, whereas sub-Saharan Africa had little or no growth. Immediately preceding the Industrial Revolution, European populations grew more rapidly than ever, except for two major declines—the Black Death devastation during the fourteenth century, and the years between 1600 and 1650, when the Thirty Years War took place. Accompanying the Industrial Revolution were declines in mortality that led to tremendous population growth for what we now call the developed world (Europe, Anglo-America, Australia, New Zealand, and Japan). The ensuing declines in fertility have led to relatively slow or no growth in these countries today. Mortality declines in developing countries, more rapid than the earlier ones in the developed world, have brought about the recent surges in population growth in most of Asia, Latin America, and Africa. Today, regional variations persist, both between the developed and developing worlds and within each sector as well.[7]

The highest rates of population increase presently are in eastern and western Africa, and the United Nations expects these increases to peak at 33 per 1,000 during the 1990s. Population growth rates in Latin America, which led the world between 1950 and 1965, have begun to decline, as have those in most parts of Asia, although both of these regions are projected to grow at annual rates of at least 10 per thousand into the next century. Population growth is close to zero now in western and northern Europe, yet remains over 1 percent annually in Australia and New Zealand, with the other developed countries experiencing growth rates intermediate to these.[8]

FRAMEWORKS FOR ANALYZING THE CAUSES OF POPULATION GROWTH

Explanations for world population growth fall into two categories. The first relates population to the means of subsistence. It is obvious that the population of the world can be no greater than that number which can provide itself with a minimum subsistence from the world's resources. Since for most of the period in which human beings have inhabited this planet, the majority have lived very close to a minimum level of subsistence, major population increase has been possible only when the means of subsistence could be increased proportionately.

A second perspective for examining the causes of world population increase examines this increase in terms of its two components, the birth rate and the death rate. On a worldwide basis, population cannot increase unless the birth rate exceeds the death rate, and the more the former exceeds the latter, the higher the rate of population growth will be. Analysis of world population growth from this framework focuses on factors leading to changes in birth and death rates.

Population Growth and the Means of Subsistence

Societies develop because human beings cannot grow to maturity independently from other persons. In turn, human societies depend on other animals, on plant species, and on such requisite features of the inanimate environment as water, air, and suitable temperature. The consequences of populations growing faster than the means of subsistence were outlined initially by Thomas Robert Malthus in 1798, in his famous essay on population.[9] The means of subsistence, Malthus claimed, grew only at an *arithmetic* rate, whereas populations tended to grow at a *geometric* rate. When the imbalance between growth in the means of subsistence and in population became too great, factors such as hunger, epidemic disease, and war—which Malthus termed *"positive checks"*—would operate to increase the death rate and reduce the population to a level compatible with the means of subsistence. In his later writings, Malthus abandoned his pessimistic dogma and expressed the hope that people could avoid higher death rates through certain *"preventive checks"*— that is, checks on the birth rate. Malthus proposed late marriage as the best means to reduce the birth rate, since he believed that any limitation of birth within marriage was immoral.[10]

One criticism of Malthus's theory is that he overlooked the importance of technology in contributing to the faster-than-arithmetic growth of the means of subsistence. Through technology and social organization, people have been able to manipulate their environment so as to increase per capita consumption and population size. As societies develop more sophisticated technologies, they can support larger populations and a higher standard of living for that population. Lenski and Lenski show how human societies have evolved through four types of technologies—hunting and gathering, horticultural and pastoral, agrarian, and industrial—and how each type of society allows for increasing numbers of people.[11]

Members of hunting and gathering societies spend most of their time searching for food—edible plants and wild animals. Such societies require large amounts of land, and after depleting the food sources in one location, they move on to another. Each society tends to be small and to be located far from other hunting and gathering societies. The family is the primary social institution in a hunting and gathering society, and all ages participate in food production. Gathering is usually done by women, while men hunt game.

The next types of society in the Lenskis' scheme are horticultural and pastoral societies. Approximately 10,000 years ago, some hunting and gathering societies began to use tools to cultivate plants, and gradually, over the next few thousand years, horticulture replaced hunting and gathering. Those hunting and gathering societies with abundant vegetation may not have found horticulture advantageous and may thus have turned to raising animals instead of plants. Pastoral societies also emerged in very dry regions where horticulture was not feasible. Some societies combined plant cultivation and animal domestication to increase the stability of their food supply. One outcome of these technologies was the possibility of a food surplus for the first time, allowing for a larger population and enabling some persons to carry out activities not related to food production; hence the emergence of merchants, teachers, and artisans.

As domesticated animals began to be used for drawing plows, agrarian societies developed, with even larger scales of food production. Other technical innovations of agrarian societies, including the wheel, metalworking, and the symbolic representation of numbers and words, meant that a society could encompass a larger population spread over a wider geographical span; the Roman Empire is one example. As agricultural productivity continued to increase, fewer individuals were needed to produce food for the entire society, making urbanization and the rise of large cities possible.

The fourth and final type of society in the Lenskis' scheme is the industrial society, one that uses inanimate sources of energy, rather than humans or animals, for production and transportation. Because of substantial increases in agricultural productivity, these societies can support an even larger population, and for the first time, urban residents outnumber rural ones. The beginnings of the industrial society in Europe coincided with Christopher Columbus's voyage to America. The explorers brought back cultivated plants previously unknown in Europe and Asia, including potatoes, maize, beans, and tomatoes. Of these plants, probably the most important to Northern Europe was the potato, because the cool and rainy summers of that region, in contrast with warmer climates, are not well suited for grain production. The potato, however, was ideal for this cooler climate, and the yield of potatoes from 1 acre of land was equivalent in food value to the yield of 2 to 4 acres sown with grain. The potato was introduced into Ireland in around 1600 and probably had its greatest impact there. By 1800, the potato was practically the sole item in the diet of the Irish masses. The reliability of the potato harvest led the population of Ireland to more than double between 1754 and 1846, from 3.2 million to 8.2 million, despite heavy out-migration to the United States and other nations.[12] A potato blight in 1845, however, led to tremendous loss in the Irish population between 1846 and 1848. Out of a population of 9 million, over 1 million persons died and an additional million or more emigrated.[13] The potato played an equally important role, although at a somewhat later date, in the other countries of Northern Europe, particularly England, the Netherlands, Scandinavia, Germany, Poland, and Russia. In Russia, from 1725 to 1858 the population increased more than threefold (within the boundaries of the former year).[14]

A hallmark of the industrial society was the steam engine, invented by James Watt in 1769. This invention signaled the beginning of the period during which energy was to come from inanimate fossilized sources (coal, petroleum, and natural gas). Numerous inventions stimulated the efficient use of inanimate energy in Europe, North America, and elsewhere, with two broad consequences. First, a series of innovations in agriculture and manufacturing made it possible for a rapidly decreasing number of persons to produce an increasing quantity of food, clothing, shelter, and other necessities of life. Second, a revolution in the costs of transportation made it possible for various regions to specialize in those goods and services that they could produce at the lowest cost and eliminated the danger of famine caused by local failures in food production.

Beyond the industrial society is the postindustrial society—one in which the service sector predominates over material goods manufacturing. High technology, particularly improvements in communication, has made this societal transition possible.[15] Societies in this stage tend to exhibit reduced population growth, although the long-term impact of postindustrial technology is not yet clear.

Population Growth and Changes in Birth and Death Rates

The second framework for analyzing population growth focuses on the factors that influence the rate of births and deaths. For most of human history, the birth rate and the death rate were both very high and were at approximately the same level, leading to little or no population growth. Of course, birth and death rates would not be exactly equal in any given year; death rates in particular tended to vary considerably from year to year, but on average, over time, population growth hovered near zero for most of human history.

Zero population growth can result from many combinations of fertility and mortality; it simply means that the number of births in a given year equals the number of deaths (assuming zero net migration). Apart from periods of extremely high mortality, the most adverse mortality conditions in human history probably resulted in a life expectancy of approximately 20 years for women, slightly lower for men. Under these conditions, fewer than one-third of all women survive to the mean age of childbearing, with half of all deaths occurring to infants and children under the age of 5. Over the long run, this low life expectancy translates into a mortality rate of 50 deaths per thousand population. Therefore, the accompanying fertility rate to produce zero population growth would be 50 births per thousand population. Those women who survive to the end of the childbearing years would have an average of 6.5 children.[16] The highest recorded fertility rates belong to the Hutterites, an Anabaptist sect living in the north-central United States and south-central Canada: 10.94 children per woman during the years from 1921 to 1930.[17]

At the other end of the vital-rates continuum, the most favorable mortality conditions known to human history are those of Japan today, where the overall life expectancy is 79 years,[18] a situation that, if continued indefinitely, would produce

an annual death rate of about 13 per thousand. With mortality this low, fertility would have to be correspondingly low in order to achieve zero population growth. A birth rate of 13 per thousand means that each woman, on average, produces 2.05 children to replace herself and her partner and to allow for the small amount of mortality that occurs before the childbearing years.

For most of human history, birth and death rates were high, although not as high as the maxim''m figures cited previously.[19] Moreover, the long-term trend of these vital rates has not been one of continuous decline, even though technological developments are supposed to improve human life. Following this logic, technology should be expected to bring about a reduction in birth and death rates, particularly the latter. There is strong evidence to the contrary, however, that the birth and death rates of hunting and gathering societies, while high, were not as high as those in horticultural and pastoral societies, or even agrarian societies. First, the relatively low population density in hunting and gathering societies mitigated the potential loss of life as a result of disease. Floods, drought, and pestilence, which could wreak tremendous loss in agricultural societies, did not have as much impact on hunting and gathering societies because they were not bound to one location. Birth rates, similarly, were probably lower in hunting and gathering societies. As these societies had to be ready to move easily in search of food, families spaced their births so that they had only one or possibly two children to carry at any one time. Children tended to breastfeed for several years because alternative foods were rather difficult to chew and digest—another important reason for families to space births, although lactation itself helps to suppress ovulation, providing contraceptive protection. In addition to extending breastfeeding, couples in these societies often abstained from sexual intercourse in order to ensure sufficient birth spacing.[20]

With the advent of agriculture, human mortality increased somewhat as the more crowded conditions made epidemics more likely; in addition, there was the possibility that natural disasters could destroy crops. It also seems probable that fertility increased as well, perhaps even more than did mortality, as a more sedentary way of life made large numbers of children easier to care for than they were in a nomadic culture. The increasing numbers of people that agriculture made possible came, not from a lower death rate, but from higher birth rates.[21] During most periods, the birth rate was slightly higher than the death rate, producing an annual population growth rate of about 5 or 10 per thousand.[22] During occasional years, however, the death rate could be extremely high, due to war, famine, disease, or natural disasters. Years of food scarcity tended to have very high death rates. Not only did food shortage sometimes cause actual starvation, but more important, it caused malnutrition and undernourishment, and under these conditions the death rate from various infectious diseases rose markedly. One of the most famous epidemics in human history was the Black Death, which occurred in Europe during the years from 1347 to 1352. An epidemic of bubonic plague began in Constantinople in 1347 and spread throughout the Mediterranean region and the European Atlantic coast during the following year. It then moved inland and continued until it struck Russia in 1352. The Black Death killed approximately one-quarter of the population of Europe, and the continent was not able to regain its former population for many years.[23]

The birth rate in agricultural societies was more stable than the death rate, although there appears to be some variation among agricultural societies in overall fertility levels as well as in the timing of births. For example, nineteenth-century European fertility averaged approximately 30 to 50 percent of the Hutterite level (3 to 5 children per woman), in part because of relatively low rates of marriage and little unmarried childbearing. Even marital fertility among most European provinces was only about three-fourths that of the Hutterites, and hence below reproductive capacity, despite the high fertility norms during that era. Moreover, cultural variations in marital customs and childbearing within marriage produced differing fertility levels within Europe itself.[24] In contrast, the agricultural societies of Asia and Latin America had fertility levels that far exceeded those of nineteenth-century Europe, primarily because of early and nearly universal marriage. Birth rates in many Asian and Latin America countries in the 1960s and 1970s exceeded 40 per thousand, and in some cases even 50 per thousand (or approximately 6 to 8 births per woman).[25]

The changes in birth and death rates that occurred with the onset of agriculture, however, were relatively small compared with the changes that accompanied industrialization. The phrase *demographic transition* refers to the changes in fertility and mortality that accompany the shift from an agricultural society to an industrial society. In an agricultural society, both birth rates and death rates are high, although birth rates tend to be relatively stable over time, while the death rates can fluctuate from year to year. *Demographic transition theory* states that in the next stage, mortality rates begin to decline, while fertility rates remain high, producing high population growth. In the third stage, fertility rates then fall, lagging behind the declining mortality rates, so that population growth continues, although not at accelerating rates. At the end of the demographic transition, both fertility and mortality are at low and fairly even levels, again producing a situation of little or no population growth. In contrast to the first stage, however, in the post-transition period mortality rates are low and constant, while fertility rates are low and fluctuating. In addition to describing the changing vital rates, demographic transition theory links this phenomenon to industrialization.[26]

Preindustrial societies are thought to have relatively little control over mortality, but they develop norms of high fertility to counteract the effects of mortality. It is in the best interest of an agricultural society to encourage childbearing so as to prevent the population from dying out over time. For individual families, high fertility is desirable in order to replace losses from infant and child mortality and to have large numbers of children who can become productive relatively early in their lives and who can provide old-age support for the parents. Furthermore, the marginal cost of an additional child tends to be low in a rural, agricultural society because of the lack of formal education and because women, the primary childcare providers, can incorporate this activity along with their other responsibilities, including farming. This stage of high, relatively constant birth rates and high, fluctuating death rates is the pretransition period.[27]

In the next stage, demographic transition theory postulates that mortality falls because of the societal changes that accompany industrialization. In Europe, the United States, Canada, Australia, New Zealand, and Japan, improvements in transportation, communication, and food production all raised the general level of nutrition. In addition, the development of sewer systems, clean water supplies, and the recognition of personal hygiene contributed to a decline in the incidence and severity of infectious disease. It is important to note that these technological advances predated those of modern medicine; the exception was the smallpox vaccine, which became available in the nineteenth century. Mortality rates continued to decline with medical advances in the prevention and treatment of infectious disease, the former through inoculation, and the latter through the use of antibiotics. Outside of the economically developed nations, death rates remained high until the end of World War II. After World War II, a very pronounced reduction of mortality in these nations—a reduction much more rapid than had ever occurred in Europe or the United States—accelerated world population growth. Some of these nations have continued to experience mortality reductions and currently have rates that are not a great deal higher than those of the more developed nations. In others, however, the level of mortality still remains distinctly higher than that of the economically developed nations.[28]

The very rapid decline of mortality rates in countries outside of Europe, Japan, Australia, New Zealand, and the United States resulted in large measure from inoculation for infectious disease, reduction of malaria through insecticide spraying, and the cure of infectious disease through antibiotics. However, a large proportion of persons in these nations continue to exist on substandard diets and live in unsanitary conditions.

The first nations to experience economic advance as a result of the scientific industrial revolution were characterized not only by declining mortality rates but also by a fall in fertility levels. Demographic transition theory stipulates that fertility decreases in response to both declining mortality and the broader socioeconomic changes that accompany industrialization, although the connections among these variables were not spelled out by the first demographic transition theorists. Beginning in the 1960s, demographers began to explore more precisely the correlates and determinants of fertility decline, using historical data from European countries that had already completed the transition and survey data collected in developing countries that were in the process of transition.

The European Fertility Project attempted to discover exactly what factors led to a fertility decline, both to understand better the historical record and to suggest the most effective policies for more rapid fertility declines in developing countries. The overall conclusion of this project, which consisted of dozens of books, articles, and reports, was that "fertility declines took place under a wide variety of social, economic, and demographic conditions."[29] While fertility usually fell only after mortality had declined, in some places, notably most of France, fertility began to fall before mortality. Industrialization appeared to be correlated with fertility decline in most European provinces, although this relationship was weak and often not statistically significant. The more modern provinces, as measured by higher levels of urbanization and education, tended to experience fertility declines earlier and faster, but again there were some exceptions. Two generalizations, however, do appear to have widespread support: First, once underway, the fertility decline was irreversible; and second, cultural factors, such as language or the status of women, affected the timing and speed of the transition.[30] The issue of fertility decline, both historically in developed countries and contemporaneously in developing countries will be discussed more fully in Chapter 4.

During the period just before World War II, the industrialized nations of Europe, North America, and Oceania had achieved fertility and mortality rates low enough to make their intrinsic rates of natural increase (eventual population growth rates without taking into account the effect of migration) zero. All of these nations were therefore considered to be in the fourth and final stage of demographic transition. Moreover, the demographic history of all these industrialized nations appeared to confirm the theory of demographic transition. All of them had experienced major long-term declines, both in mortality and in fertility, with the decline in mortality generally preceding the decline in fertility. Furthermore, if one looked at the nations of the world in cross-sectional perspective, all of the developed nations with low fertility and mortality rates contrasted sharply with the less developed nations, all experiencing high fertility, and most of them, high mortality.

In the years following World War II, however, events cast increasing doubt on the the classic statement of the demographic transition with respect to fertility. Demographers with faith in the theory of the demographic transition could not at first believe that fertility in the United States was actually rising to a level higher than that which had existed before World War II. At first the observed postwar jump in the birth rate was explained by the theory that births had been temporarily postponed because of World War II. When fertility continued to increase in the United States well into the 1950s, however, the postwar explanation was not sufficient. Demographers instead examined the effect of changes in age at marriage and the intervals between births. Whelpton showed that a decline in age at marriage and in the maternal age at which children were born could result in a temporary inflation of the annual fertility measures even though there was no change in the average number of children per woman completing the reproductive period.[31] Because the United States did experience a pronounced post – World War II decline in the age at marriage and in the intervals between marriage and the birth of each child, it could plausibly be argued that the size of completed families in the United States was not rising. Only by the late 1950s had sufficient data accumulated to prove conclusively that the size of completed families in the United States among recent marriage cohorts was significantly above the level attained by those women who were married in the decade before World War II.[32]

Demographers were then faced with the embarrassing realization that fertility in the United States had increased despite the projection that fertility would not rise once the final stage of demographic transition had been reached. Moreover, fertility had risen in a period that had seen increased industrialization, increased urbanization, increased education, and a dramatic rise in the level of economic development.

Since the late 1950s, the U.S. baby boom has been viewed in a longer-term perspective—as a temporary upswing in an otherwise long-term decline. This interpretation coincides with the demographic transition theory's prediction of fertility in a post-transition society—namely, that it will be low and fluctuating, in response to social and economic trends. There does seem to be some evidence that although economic development brings about lower fertility in the long run, favorable economic conditions can cause a rise in fertility in the short run.[33]

In general, the demographic transition theory has proven to be a useful tool for explaining the changes in fertility and mortality rates of the past. More of the so-called developing societies are well under way in their demographic transitions, experiencing mortality and fertility declines. One part of the demographic transition that has not been questioned until recently is the future course of mortality in a post-transition society. It may be possible for mortality to decline even further than the already low levels in developed countries. Another possibility is that mortality will increase, perhaps due to the effect of a particularly virulent disease, such as acquired immune deficiency syndrome (AIDS), or due to environmental changes that could adversely affect the food supply.

While much demographic research has attempted to uncover and explain changes in population growth and size, these variables are not the only aspects of human population structure. Another important structural variable is population distribution, the topic of Chapter 2.

NOTES

1. Coale, Ansley J., "The History of the Human Population," *The Human Population* "A Scientific American Book" (San Francisco: W. H. Freeman and Company), 1974 pp. 16–25.
2. Tanner, Nancy Makepeace, *On Becoming Human* (Cambridge: Cambridge University Press, 1981).
3. Campbell, Bernard, ed., *Humankind Emerging*, 4th ed. (Boston: Little, Brown, and Company, 1985).
4. Lancaster, Jane, and Chet Lancaster, "Parental Investment: The Hominid Adaptation," in *How Humans Adapt: A Biocultural Odyssey*, ed. D. Ortner (Washington, DC: Smithsonian Institution Press, 1983).
5. Deevey, Edward S., Jr., "The Human Population," *Scientific American* (September 1960), 203, 3, 195–204.
6. Estimates of population and growth rates from 8000 B.C. to A.D. 1 are from Ansley J. Coale, "The History of the Human Population"; *The Human Population* "A Scientific American Book" (San Francisco: W. H. Freeman and Company), 1974. Population and growth rate estimates from 1650 to 1900 are from Carr-Saunders, A. M., *World Population: Past Growth and Present Trends* (Oxford: Clarendon, 1936), p. 42. Population estimates from 1950 to 2025 are from United Nations, Department of International Economic and Social Affairs, *World Population Prospects 1988* (New York: United Nations, 1989), p. 28.

7. Menard, Scott W., "Regional Variations in Population Histories," in *Perspectives on Population*, eds. Scott W. Menard and Elizabeth W. Moen (New York: Oxford University Press, 1987), pp. 10–15.
8. United Nations, *World Population Prospects*, pp. 30–37.
9. Malthus, Thomas Robert, *Population: The First Essay* (Ann Arbor: Ann Arbor Paperbacks, 1959).
10. Malthus, Thomas, "A Summary View of the Principle of Population," in *Three Essays on Population*, eds. Thomas Malthus, Julian Huxley, and Frederick Osborn (New York: Mentor Books, 1960), pp. 13–59.
11. Lenski, Gerhard, and Jean Lenski, *Human Societies: An Introduction to Macrosociology*, 5th ed. (New York: McGraw-Hill, 1987), p. 75; and Walter Goldschmidt, *Man's Way* (Cleveland: World, 1959), pp. 181–218.
12. Langer, William L., "Europe's Initial Population Explosion," *The American Historical Review*, 69, 1 (October 1963), 1–17.
13. Rubenstein, Richard, *The Age of Triage* (Boston: Beacon Press, 1983), pp. 98–101.
14. Langer, "Europe's Initial Population Explosion," 1–17.
15. Bell, Daniel, *The Coming of Postindustrial Society* (New York: Basic Books, 1976).
16. Coale, "The History of the Human Population," pp. 16–25.
17. Coale, Ansley J., and Roy Treadway, "Summary of the Changing Distribution," in *The Decline of Fertility in Europe*, eds. Ansley J. Coale and Susan Cotts Watkins (Princeton, NJ: Princeton University Press, 1986), pp. 31–181.
18. Haub, Carl, Mary M. Kent, Machiko Yanagishita, "1990 World Population Data Sheet" (Washington, DC: Population Reference Bureau, 1990).
19. Davis, Kingsley, "The History of Birth and Death," *Bulletin of the Atomic Scientists*, 42, 4 (April 1986), 20–23, provides examples throughout early human history of moderately high fertility and mortality rates. John Bongaarts, "Why High Birth Rates Are So Low," *Population and Development Review*, 1, 2 (December 1975), 289–296, outlines biological and social factors that have kept fertility well below the theoretical upper limits.
20. For a more elaborate explanation of fertility and mortality in preagricultural societies, see Dumond, Don, "The Limitation of Human Population: A Natural History," *Science*, 187 (February 28, 1975), 713–721; and Ansley Coale, "History of the Human Population." The practices associated with extended birth intervals are analyzed in Lesthaeghe, Ronald, and Hilary Page, eds., *Child-Spacing in Tropical Africa: Traditions and Change* (London: Academic Press, 1981).
21. Coale, "The History of the Human Population."
22. Cipolla, Carlo M., *The Economic History of World Population*, 6th ed. (Middlesex, England: Penguin Books, 1975), p. 78.
23. Petersen, William, *Population*, 2nd ed. (New York: Macmillan, 1969), pp. 388–91.
24. Watkins, Susan, "Conclusions," in *The Decline of Fertility in Europe*, eds. Coale and Watkins, pp. 420–49.
25. Teitelbaum, Michael, "Relevance of Demographic Transition Theory for Developing Countries," *Science*, 188 (May 2, 1975), 420–425.
26. Thompson, Warren S., *Population and Peace in the Pacific* (Chicago: University of Chicago Press, 1946), pp. 22–35; C. P. Blacker, "Stages in Population Growth," *Eugenics Review*, 39, 3 (October 1947), 88–102; Kingsley Davis, *Human Society* (New York: Macmillan, 1949), pp. 603–8; and Frank W. Notestein, "The Economics of Population and Food Supplies," in *Proceedings of the Eighth International Conference of Agricultural Economists* (London: Oxford University Press, 1953), pp. 15–31.
27. Coale, Ansley J., and Edgar M. Hoover, *Population and Economic Development in Low-Income Countries* (Princeton, NJ: Princeton University Press, 1958), pp. 9–17.
28. On the decline of mortality in Europe, see Glass, David V., and D. E. C. Eversley, eds., *Population in History* (Chicago: Aldine, 1965); and for a general discussion of trends

in mortality in various areas of the world, see The World Bank, *World Development Report 1984* (New York: Oxford University Press, 1984), pp. 56–74.

29. Knodel, John, and Etienne van de Walle, "Lessons from the Past: Policy Implications of Historical Fertility Studies," *The Decline of Fertility in Europe*, eds. Coale and Watkins, pp. 390–419.

30. See Watkins, "Conclusions," pp. 420–449; and Knodel and van de Walle, "Lessons from the Past."

31. Whelpton, Pascal K., *Cohort Fertility: Native White Women in the United States* (Princeton, NJ: Princeton University Press, 1954).

32. U.S. Bureau of the Census, "Fertility of the Population: March 1957," *Current Population Reports*, series P-20, no. 84 (August 8, 1958).

33. For historical evidence of a rise in fertility associated with economic development, see Krause, J. T., "Some Implications of Recent Work in Historical Demography," *Comparative Studies in Society and History*, 1, 2 (January 1957), 164–88; Habakkuk, H. J., "English Population in the Eighteenth Century," *Economic History Review*, 6, 2 (December 1953), 117–33; Petersen, William, "The Demographic Transition in the Netherlands," *American Sociological Review*, 25, 3 (June 1960), 334–47. Easterlin, Richard, *Birth and Fortune: The Impact of Numbers on Personal Welfare* (New York: Basic Books, 1980); and Ryder, Norman B., "The Future of American Fertility," *Social Problems*, 26, 3 (February 1979), 359–370, provide explanations for periodic changes in American fertility patterns.

CHAPTER 2
THE GEOGRAPHIC DISTRIBUTION OF HUMAN POPULATIONS

THE GENERAL DISTRIBUTION OF THE WORLD'S POPULATION

Despite their flexibility in adapting to many different environments, human beings have found certain environments much more congenial than others. As a result, vast areas of land have either a scanty population or none at all. Antarctica is perhaps the most conspicuous example of a large land area that has no permanent human inhabitants. Other sparsely populated areas of the world are found in the arctic zones of North America and Asia, the vast desert region extending from northern Africa through central Asia, the arid interior of Australia, and the mountainous areas in North and South America and Africa. The most densely populated areas of the world are in southern Asia, eastern Asia, western Europe, and eastern North America. Figure 2–1 shows metropolitan areas with 1 million or more persons in 1987, which is an approximate indicator of population density. Because developing countries tend to have more densely populated rural areas and proportionately fewer large metropolitan areas, actual population density is somewhat greater in some developing countries than Figure 2–1 suggests.[1]

Behind this unequal distribution of world population lie environmental and historical factors. The ideal distribution of population reflects not only the current environmental factors, but also the historical patterns of residence. Once a place becomes densely settled, it will continue to attract a large population even if the original reasons for its desirability no longer pertain. The environmental factors affecting population distribution at a given point in time are (1) climate, (2) location of water, soil, energy, and mineral resources, (3) transport relationships, and (4) historical patterns of residence.

Metropolitan Areas with Population of One Million or More

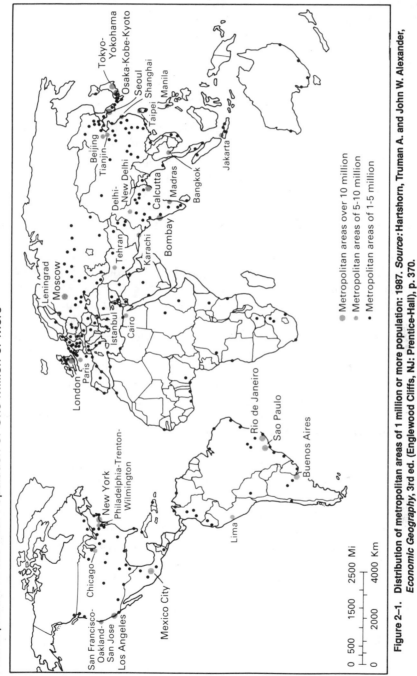

Figure 2–1. Distribution of metropolitan areas of 1 million or more population: 1987. *Source:* Hartshorn, Truman A. and John W. Alexander, *Economic Geography*, 3rd ed. (Englewood Cliffs, NJ: Prentice-Hall), p. 370.

● Metropolitan areas over 10 million
● Metropolitan areas of 5-10 million
• Metropolitan areas of 1-5 million

Climate bears some rather obvious relationships to population distribution. Large parts of the world attract either no people at all or at best only a few hardy or adventurous ones because of the temperature. Desirable metropolitan areas to live in the United States on the basis of climate favor those places with mild temperatures and limited extreme temperatures. Less desirable metropolitan areas suffer from very cold winters or hot, humid summers.[2] While generous rainfall might not be very desirable for metropolitan residents, it would be essential for most agriculture, illustrating how "tastes" in climate can vary.

Of course, even a large metropolitan area requires large quantities of water for human consumption and for manufacturing. If rainfall is deficient, a dense population can be maintained only if there is abundant groundwater, a large nearby river, facilities for transporting water inexpensively by pipeline or aqueduct, or processing plants for the inexpensive desalinization of seawater.

The quality of soil under cultivation is also an important determinant of population distribution. The three best soils are (1) alluvial deposits in river valleys, (2) volcanic soils, and (3) the chernozem (black earth) soils of certain temperate grasslands. Soils such as these are capable of producing large quantities of food per acre and hence can support quite dense populations. The soils of poorest quality are the latosols (leached red and yellow), covering much of tropic Africa and Latin America, and the podzolic (organic/mineral-ashy) soils of the arctic and subarctic regions. In these areas, population is usually sparse. The absence of soil, as in mountainous regions of rock surface, is an even more severe inhibitor of high population density.

A mineral or energy resource may also attract population. If such resources are to be exploited, the population must be at least large enough to provide the labor force necessary for mining or extraction. If the resource is bulky, additional numbers of people may move nearby because it is often more profitable to use the resource where it is taken from the earth than elsewhere. Thus, iron and steel industries often tend to locate near coal mines because a large amount of coal is used in manufacturing iron and steel. In turn, an area with a large iron and steel industry tends to attract so many manufacturers of fabricated metal products that a coal-mining area often becomes a major center of heavy industry.

The third environmental determinant of population distribution is transport relationships. Since almost all of the resources for human subsistence can be used at some site other than that in which they are found in nature, certain areas may become important centers of population if their costs of transport from resource areas to market areas are low. With present technology, water transport is usually much less costly than transportation by land. Hence coastal areas and islands are apt to be areas that can cheaply assemble raw materials from elsewhere, process them, and ship the finished product to other markets. England exemplifies an area with very favorable transport relationships. Countries with a rugged terrain, such as Mexico and Colombia, have poor transport relationships because the costs of highway and railroad construction are so high. Similarly, transport relationships are poor in land-locked nations situated at great distances from markets or resource areas.

Once an area becomes densely populated, it stands a good chance of retaining a transport advantage over more thinly populated competitive regions in marketing its produce, and this factor alone will continue to attract people. The northeast coast of the United States might not prove to be the most populous location if the United States were suddenly depopulated and could be populated again, but the present concentration of population there stems in part from its relative proximity to Europe. The northeast gained a transportation advantage by attracting both the bulk of the first European settlers and the lion's share of the early market-produce business.

New York City's current size certainly reflects its past environmental advantages. New York's port does not now have any noticeable intrinsic advantage over those in Norfolk, Baltimore, or Philadelphia; all of these are closer to America's heartland. What gave New York its greatest advantage over its competitors was the the Erie Canal, completed in 1825. Upon the canal's opening, the freight rate from Buffalo to New York declined from $100 to $10 a ton, and travel time from 15 to 6 days.[3] As a result, the population of New York City soon outstripped that of its principal rivals (Baltimore, Philadelphia, and Boston), which, without canals, did not have inexpensive access to the interior. Today railroads and highways are New York's chief links to the hinterlands, and New York no longer has an advantage in transporting goods to and from inland America. Because of the great lead in population that it attained as a result of the Erie Canal, however, New York City was able to maintain its premier position on the northeast coast.

Because dense populations tend to maintain themselves, past social policies that helped to determine these densities are important in explaining current population densities. For example, although Brazilia became the capital of Brazil in the 1960s, Rio de Janeiro, the previous seat of government, continues to have a much larger population, mainly because it was Brazil's capital for so many years. In addition to the choice of the capital city, other social policies that can determine population distribution within a nation include tariffs, agricultural subsidies, and land development policies. The current population distribution among nations is also influenced by such past and present social policies as warfare and restrictions on international migration.

Changes in population distribution result from several factors. In the very long run, they may be due to environmental changes, but these usually occur very slowly and hence are not important to short-run changes in population distribution. Changes in technology, population growth rates, and social policy are probably the most important determinants of short-term shifts in population distribution.

WORLD URBANIZATION

One of the most striking changes in many nations over the last 200 years has been that in the proportion of population living in cities—a change termed *urbanization.* The proportion of the total world population living in urban areas grew from 29 percent in 1950 to over 40 percent by 1985 and is expected to climb above 60 percent by 2025.[4] Urbanization has been closely associated with economic development. In the history of the now-developed nations, each increase in material well-being was associated with a greater proportion of the total population living in urban areas. For example, in the United States the proportion of all persons classified as urban residents increased from 5.1 percent in 1790 to 73.7 percent in 1980.[5] A large gap remains between the more developed and less developed countries in their levels of urbanization. In 1985, approximately one-third of the populations of the less developed countries resided in urban areas, as compared with approximately three-fourths of the populations of more developed countries.[6] Despite the relatively lower levels of overall urbanization in the developing countries, seven of the ten largest urban agglomerations in the world are in developing countries. Mexico City is projected to be the largest urban agglomeration in the twenty-first century.[7]

The urbanization of the world during the last 200 years has had two fundamental causes. First, as a nation becomes more wealthy, its inhabitants spend less of their income on food and more on other goods and services. Consumer goods other than food are almost invariably produced more cheaply in cities than in the countryside, both because cities are centers of transportation and thus can assemble raw materials and ship out a finished product at a relatively low cost, and because cities can provide a labor force sufficient to produce commodities by mass production—a method that in most cases results in less expensive costs all around. Cities are also the best locations for many specialized services, such as wholesale trade, higher education, hospitals, banking, and insurance. Because cities can provide many services that rural areas cannot, they often attract people who might have equal or better economic opportunities elsewhere. Hence, urban economic opportunity stimulates urbanization, and urbanization in turn stimulates the economic opportunity available in cities.

The second major reason for urbanization has been the changing character of food production. Before the Industrial Revolution, only a few input goods were necessary to produce agricultural commodities. Today, at least in the more developed nations, the situation is very different. To create their produce, farmers increasingly rely on artificial fertilizers, insecticides, machinery, and inanimate sources of energy. These many inputs to agricultural production cannot be produced directly on the farm, but instead are usually produced in urban centers. As a result, a large part of "farm" work is now done, not on the farm, but in urban areas. Furthermore, for the many persons in the developed nations who do not themselves live on farms, food that remains on the farm is of no direct use. Farm produce must be transported from the farm, processed, and then distributed for urban consumption, and urban residents typically carry out these additional activities.

Concomitant with increasing urbanization in the developed nations has been a phenomenon called *suburbanization.* Suburbanization most commonly means an increase in the proportion of the total population in a metropolis that lives outside the official limits of the central city of that metropolis. In the United States and other developed nations, recent decades have witnessed a much more rapid growth in the political areas of the metropolis outside the central city than within its bounds. Suburbanization, however, can also take place within the central city itself, as there is a tendency for the parts of the metropolis nearest the central business district to decline in population while those most removed from the central business district increase dramatically. Another form of suburbanization involves formerly nonmetropolitan areas gaining enough population to be reclassified as metropolitan, either by increasing the boundaries of existing metropolitan areas or by creating new metropolitan areas. Metropolitan growth increased continually after World War II, and most of this growth occurred through suburbanization, as the central cities of most U.S. metropolitan areas lost population to the surrounding suburbs. This trend of deconcentration within metropolitan areas continued in the 1970s with the inner suburbs losing population as well, while the outlying suburbs grew. Urban areas became geographically larger but less densely populated.[8] During the 1970s, for the first time in the twentieth century, nonmetropolitan areas grew faster than metropolitan areas, as the overall American population became less densely settled. By the mid-1980s, however, metropolitan population growth began to overtake nonmetropolitan growth again.[9]

The shift of population away from central cities to suburban areas has several causes. The first is that residential use of land must compete with other land uses. Increasingly, land adjacent to the central business district is taken over for expressways, parking lots, and commercial use, and as a result, residential density declines.

A second cause involves changes in the demand for residential space brought about by changes in income, the number of leisure hours, and the cost of travel. Larger incomes have allowed larger proportions of more salaries to be spent on travel to and from work, and shorter workdays have given the commuter more time for such travel. In addition, the automobile has greatly reduced the cost and time of commuting between the central city and suburban areas, some of which are remote enough not to be linked to the central city by public transport. Further, families have moved out of the areas adjacent to the central business districts to escape high land costs, soaring rents, and general lack of elbowroom.

Third, with an increasing volume of goods shipped by truck rather than by railroad, and with a rising proportion of workers commuting by automobile rather than by public transportation, it has also been possible for a larger proportion of factories to locate away from the central business district. An increasing dispersion of jobs also reinforces a dispersion of residence.

A fourth cause for declining central city growth relates to the quality of existing city housing and the rise in per capita income. In the areas adjacent to the central business district, housing is generally rather crowded. As the average income of the population of the inner-city area increases, the residents wish to spend more money on housing. The usual pattern is one of demanding more space per capita. Households remaining in the city might convert a two-family dwelling to a single-family home, but more typically, they move to the suburbs.

While the more developed nations tend to have multiple urban centers, urbanization patterns in the developing world favor the growth of large urban agglomerations, with one metropolitan area often serving as the primary urban location for an entire country. In 1955, 18 percent of South Korea's 21.5 million population lived in or near Seoul, but by 1980, when the population grew to 37.4 million, 36 percent of the country resided in the Seoul metropolitan area. The growth of these urban "core" regions in developing nations poses serious threats to the infrastructure (for example, transportation, sanitation) and to the physical environment, as they produce large amounts of air and water pollution. Growth of large urban agglomerations will continue to be greater among developing countries.[10]

We have seen in these first two chapters how modernization has brought about changes in population structure—increasing both size and density. In the following chapter we will examine the effect that population has, in turn, on the physical environment.

NOTES

1. Davis, Kingsley, "Asia's Cities: Problems and Options," *Population and Development Review*, 1, 1 (September 1975), 71–86; Vining, Daniel, "The Growth of Core Regions in the Third World," *Scientific American*, 252, 4 (April 1985), 42–49.
2. Boyer, Richard, and David Savageau, *Places Rated Almanac*, 2nd ed. (Chicago: Rand McNally and Company, 1985), pp. 4–5.
3. *Encyclopaedia Britannica*, 1965, s.v. "Erie Canal."
4. United Nations, Department of International Economic and Social Affairs, *The Prospects of World Urbanization, 1988*, Population Studies No. 112 (New York: United Nations, 1989), p. 4.
5. U.S. Bureau of the Census, *Historical Statistics of the United States: Colonial Times to 1970*, bicentennial ed., part 2. (Washington, DC: U.S. Government Printing Office, 1975), p. 12; and U.S. Bureau of the Census, *Statistical Abstract of the United States 1990* (Washington, DC: U.S. Government Printing Office, 1990), p. 17.
6. United Nations, *World Urbanization*, p. 4.
7. Ibid., p. 19.
8. Long, Larry, and Diana DeAre, "The Slowing of Urbanization in the U.S.," *Scientific American*, 249, 1 (July 1983), 33–41.
9. Long, Larry, and Diana DeAre, "U.S. Population Redistribution: A Perspective on the Nonmetropolitan Turnaround," *Population and Development Review*, 14, 3 (September 1988), 433–450.
10. Vining, Daniel R., Jr., "The Growth of Core Regions in the Third World," *Scientific American*, 252, 4 (April 1985), 42–49; and United Nations, *World Urbanization*, pp. 22–25.

CHAPTER 3
HUMAN SOCIETIES AND THEIR ENVIRONMENTAL CONSTRAINTS

Technology can change the carrying capacity of the environment and has allowed increasing numbers of humans to inhabit the earth. In the last two chapters we addressed population size, growth, and distribution as outcomes of technological evolution. In this chapter we will examine how human populations have affected the environment. In addition to population size, growth, and distribution, consumption patterns can make an impact on the environment. We will examine six direct effects of population on the environment and how these have led to global warming, a decline in food productivity, and the extinction of plant and animal species. The chapter concludes with a discussion of the prospects for human survival and the quality of life.

HUMAN CONSUMPTION PATTERNS

Both population growth and human consumption patterns have contributed to environmental degradation. Changing consumption patterns over time as well as differential use in more recent times have led to a situation that cannot continue beyond the short term.

As technological innovation allowed humanity to move from hunting and gathering societies to agricultural societies to industrial societies, human beings increasingly depended on nonrenewable resources instead of renewable resources. For most of their history, people used other living organisms—plants and animals—for food, shelter, clothing, tools, and fuel. Agriculture made it possible for human society to overuse natural resources, by, for example, allowing topsoil to erode or accumulate salts through extended irrigation. Before industrialization, humans used renewable sources of energy, both animate (for example, horse-drawn plows) and inanimate (wind or water power). From the beginning, industrialization relied upon nonrenewable sources of energy, primarily fossil fuels. The first of these energy sources was coal; then petroleum and natural gas became feasible and eventually more desirable.[1] In recent years coal production has increased slowly in the more developed countries, but more rapidly in many of the developing countries, most notably China and India.

The increasing number of vehicles, particularly diesel-fueled ones, which spew suspended particulate matter into the air, compounds air pollution problems in developing countries. Even in Europe, the growing number of diesel-fueled vehicles may wipe out the gains of earlier legislation to control air pollution. Despite some of the strictest air-quality controls in the United States, California has not been able to control the burgeoning number of automotive vehicles, due to both rapid population growth in the state and increasing number of cars per capita.[2]

Across the United States, more workers are driving to their jobs from one suburb to another than from the suburbs to the central city. Public transportation routes, which typically radiate outward along spokes from the central city, are not changing fast enough to meet the new commuting patterns.[3]

Another example of changing consumption patterns is the expansion of waste products. While the U.S. population increased by one-third between 1960 and 1986, household and commercial waste rose 80 percent, because of a growing preference for disposable products and extraneous packaging materials. The amount of plastic trash alone expanded from 400,000 tons in 1960 to 10 million tons in 1986.[4]

Not only has energy use changed over human history, but in a parallel fashion, human food consumption has also undergone dramatic transformations. Early hunters and gatherers subsisted on a diet of meat or fish, along with edible plants they could collect. Societies living in areas with plentiful animal supplies emphasized meat or fish in their diets, while other human societies probably ate animal products only occasionally. As humans began to develop horticultural techniques, animal products became a relatively minor part of the human diet. Staple grains (especially rice, corn, and wheat), supplemented with occasional animal products, legumes, fruits, and nuts, constituted the major food source for most agricultural societies.[5]

Industrialization initially worsened the human diet as people left rural food producing areas for crowded cities. Eventually, several technological advances that accompanied industrialization—transportation, refrigeration, and canning—made a more varied diet possible. Improved transportation meant that more foods were available and that they arrived in better condition. Refrigeration and canning allowed people to store food for extended periods, which also improved the variety and quality of the diet.[6] These technologies, however, have made major environmental impacts. Transporting food involves burning of fossil fuels, whether goods are shipped by air, rail, sea, or road. Artificial refrigeration releases chlorofluorocarbons (CFCs) into the air, contributing to global warming and to a dangerous reduction of ozone in the stratosphere.

One of the major dietary changes for more developed countries is the strong reliance on meat and other animal products. Instead of being consumed directly, grain goes first to feed livestock, which provide meat, eggs, and dairy products. In the 1980s, close to one-third of the global grain production went to animals.[7]

While the populations in developed countries, on average, have been over-consuming food, the average person living in 46 countries in 1985 did not consume enough calories for productive work or basic health. South Asia and Africa had the greatest numbers and proportions of hungry people. In sub-Saharan Africa, 150 million persons, or 44 percent of the total population, could not eat adequately, and 90 million of them ate so little that their growth was stunted and they were subject to severe health risks. Half of South Asia's population, 470 billion persons, did not have enough food to maintain normal activity. Unequal food distribution is both a regional issue and a matter of concern within countries as well. During the 1970s the proportion of persons with hunger declined somewhat, but because populations grew, the absolute numbers of hungry continued to rise.[8]

While human societies throughout history have displayed inequality in terms of resource use, the current chasm between the more developed and less developed worlds illustrates even more strikingly the need to reverse these trends. First, the distinction between the "more developed" and "less developed" or "developing" worlds is somewhat artificial, and should be considered a continuum rather than two discrete states. Since the 1970s, quite a few countries in Asia and some in Latin America moved closer to the "more developed" end of the spectrum than the "less developed" one. Even more important, within all countries consumption inequality exists to some extent. The developing countries include segments of society whose living standards resemble that of the average person in a more developed country. Likewise, not all members of more developed societies have access to high levels of consumption. Nevertheless, distinguishing countries into "more developed" and "developing" can still uncover sharp contrasts. Approximately 1 billion persons live in more developed nations where per capita wealth is 15 times that in the developing nations, where 4 billion persons live. Almost 1 billion of these persons suffer from malnutrition levels extreme enough to affect their health and growth.[9]

The more developed nations also consume far more energy per capita, using up nonrenewable sources and unleashing dangerous substances into the environment as by-products. Just over 5 tons of carbon per capita were emitted by the United States, as compared with less than 1 ton per capita by Mexico.[10]

ENVIRONMENTAL EFFECTS

Air Pollution

Air pollution was first recognized as a possible health hazard during the industrial revolution in Europe and the United States when smoke from coal burning filled the skies, causing illness and even death. Pollution produces suspended particles not only in the air, but also in precipitation, such as acid rain. In response to the recognition of this problem, many governments passed legislation to control the emission of sulfur dioxide and other poisonous gases from industrial plants and homes. Such efforts have met with considerable success. Public policies dealing with air pollution must often transcend state, regional, and even international borders, because prevailing winds take toxic particles from one place to another. Despite some improvements, the growing number of vehicles, particularly diesel-fueled ones, which spew suspended particulate matter into the air, will compound air pollution problems in developing countries. Breathing the air in Bombay, India, for example, has been estimated as equivalent to smoking ten cigarettes per day. In the late 1980s, over 600 million persons were breathing air with unhealthy levels of sulfur dioxide, and more than 1 billion individuals were exposed to dangerous levels of suspended particulates.[11] In April of 1986, two explosions destroyed a nuclear power reactor at Chernobyl in the Soviet Union, resulting in the highest levels of radioactivity ever recorded in many parts of Europe, with lesser pollution to the air in other northern latitudes. The immediate effects of this accident included 31 deaths, at least 1,000 injuries, and several billion dollars in damages; in the long run, the disaster could claim as many as 100,000 additional lives lost to cancer.[12]

Since the 1970 Clean Air Act was passed in the United States, carbon monoxide decreased 39 percent, and lead by 96 percent, although by 1990 over 100 million Americans were still living in places that failed Environmental Protection Agency (EPA) standards for clean air at some time during the year. Government intervention has not always been enough to combat air pollution. Despite stringent automobile exhaust laws, nearly all of California's population (96 percent) continues to breathe unhealthy air. The rapid population growth in California and the even more rapid increase in the number of automobiles have limited the effectiveness of antipollution regulations.[13]

Deforestation

Approximately one-fifth of the Earth's land surface consists of closed forests (lands where the trees retain close proximity to one another, providing uninterrupted coverage), with approximately 40 percent in the tropics and the remainder in temperate zones. Closed forests do not include open woodland areas or lands with regrowth that previously had been cleared, because tree density in these places tends to be low. More than half of these forest lands are in just four countries—the Soviet Union, Brazil, Canada, and the United States. In addition to closed forests, another 10 to 15 percent of land surface comprises woodland areas where forestland had been cleared for cultivation but then abandoned, allowing for regrowth. In recent decades, artificial plantations have slightly increased temperate forest area; however, the tropical moist forests, which include both tropical rain forests and moist deciduous forests, have been declining at dramatic rates.[14]

Deforestation of tropical moist forests takes place in order to clear land for growing crops to feed people, for cash crops (like coffee or rubber), or to provide grazing land for cattle—the latter two for export. Some countries promote deforestation, but much of it occurs without any government regulation. Typically, the trees and other biomass are cut down, allowed to dry out, then burned—hence the term "slash-and-burn deforestation." Each year approximately 6.1 million hectares of tropical moist forests are cleared, and if these rates continue, the total area would disappear in 177 years. The average rate of deforestation is 0.6 percent annually, but in some countries including Costa Rica and Sri Lanka, the rate has passed 3.0 percent, and the tropical moist forests in Nigeria and Cote d'Ivoire have declined at a rate of 5.2 percent annually.[15]

Land Pollution and Land Degradation

Land pollution and land degradation did not begin with industrialization. Ancient Mesopotamians, using faulty irrigation techniques, salinized extensive farmlands and then simply migrated to unoccupied areas. More recently, Brazilian farmers have depleted the soil of long-standing agricultural nutrients. They contributed to soil erosion through overfarming practices and then moved to tropical rainforest areas to create arable land through slash-and-burn techniques. Because rainforests tend to have thin topsoils, slash-and-burn farming practices quickly exhaust these lands, leading the farmers to proceed to other parcels of rainforests.[16]

Mountain regions face the enemy of gravity, which constantly threatens vegetation and soil. Overgrazing of livestock in the Andes, for example, has led to the desertification of what had been agriculturally productive land. As the mountain soils and vegetation have eroded, the valleys below have been subjected to the risk of floods. Desertification has also taken place in flatlands, such as in sub-Saharan Africa, where intensive farming, fuelwood gathering, and overgrazing have also stripped the land of agricultural necessities.[17]

Poor irrigation practices have continued throughout human history, but today there are no empty areas for people to occupy once they have degraded previous farmlands. In the 1980s, close to three-fourths of the food production in China came from irrigated land, while irrigation contributed to more than half of the food production in India and Indonesia. In many parts of these countries, ineffective soil drainage has led to salinization, alkalinization, and waterlogging.[18]

Depletion of Nonrenewable and Renewable Energy Sources

Energy production continued to increase during the late 1980s, but at slower rates than previously. If 1986 production levels continued, coal reserves would last 220 years, while natural gas and oil would last only 59 years and 33 years, respectively. Nuclear power use also continued to grow, although the 1986 Chernobyl accident will no doubt result in lower rates of growth. The relatively low prices of oil and other nonrenewable energy sources have constrained the economic feasibility of renewable energy sources, such as wind, water, and the sun. Fuelwood, traditionally considered a renewable energy source, was the prime energy source for almost half of the world's people in the 1980s. In some places, particularly sub-Saharan Africa, consumption of fuelwood has been outstripping the supply and contributing to environmental degradation.[19]

Water Quality and Availability

Fresh water is essential for human survival and economic development, yet access to clean water supplies is far from even. Sparsely populated countries with abundant supplies, such as Canada, New Zealand, and Iceland, have one hundred times the per capita amounts available in the arid Middle East and North Africa. Most countries are subject to either national or local water shortages, and therefore have developed techniques to manage their water supplies. Dams capture flood waters, while wells can pull up groundwater, two means to increasing water availability. Irrigation accounts for 70 percent of the world's water use, and increasing its efficiency could save quantities of water and reduce salinization and water logging on areas with bad drainage, such as the San Joaquin Valley in California. Pollution of fresh water has grown beyond local or national politics to become an issue of international concern, as countries located upstream can dump pollutants into a river, affecting another country's water supply. Disputes over water in the Middle East could likely surpass those over oil, as important rivers, such as the Euphrates, the Jordan, and the Nile, serve several nations.[20]

OUTCOMES

Global Warming

The beginning of the industrial revolution initiated a trend of increasing levels of carbon dioxide in the Earth's atmosphere. Burning fossil fuels for energy produces carbon dioxide, while deforestation releases carbon dioxide when the forests are burned. These two activities have increased the level of carbon dioxide in the atmosphere by 25 percent. Even though carbon dioxide composes less than one-thirtieth of 1 percent of the Earth's atmosphere, it is a major factor in determining the Earth's climate, along with other gases, such as methane and the CFCs. These "greenhouse gases" let sunlight into the atmosphere but prevent heat from escaping. Greenhouse gases serve an important function: Without them, our planet would be 33 degrees colder. The increasing levels of carbon dioxide and the other gases, however, will undoubtedly warm the planet over the next century. Researchers disagree, however, on the extent and speed of the warming. Estimates range from 1 or 2 degrees Centigrade up to 5 or 6 degrees Centigrade. To put these numbers in context, temperatures during the peak of the last ice age 18,000 years ago were approximately 5 degrees colder on average. Furthermore, these projections are averages for the planet. Scientists agree that there is considerable variation in warming trends, but they cannot point to definitive patterns because no one knows precisely what the role of clouds and oceans would be with an increase of carbon dioxide. For example, Iowa might become warmer and drier, making it unviable for wheat agriculture, and Manitoba, Canada, further north, would become a more hospitable climate for such agriculture. Parts of the world that are currently hot and dry—drought-stricken parts of Africa for example—might become more humid and hence more fertile. With rising temperatures, sea levels are expected to rise between 0.2 and 1.5 meters due to glacier and ice melting and thermal expansion of the oceans, endangering coastal areas.[21]

Food Productivity Decline

Global food production was able to keep up with or surpass population growth between 1950 and 1984, although there have been local exceptions—a major famine in China around 1960, for example, and declines in food production in sub-Saharan Africa since 1970. The Green Revolution, referring to the development of high-yielding strains of wheat and rice, helped boost food production between 1950 and 1965. Two other factors—irrigation and chemical fertilizers—joined with the Green Revolution to make the 1984 grain production yield 2.6 times that of 1950, an unprecedented increase, and possibly not to be duplicated in the future.[22]

The problem of food productivity is particularly acute in Africa. In the 1960s, agricultural productivity increased along with population growth. Beginning in the 1970s, however, per capita food production fell in Africa by about 1 percent per year. In the early 1980s, per capita food production plummeted 10 percent. It increased slightly during the latter part of the 1980s, but not enough to compensate for the tremendous population growth in Africa.[23]

Is there enough food to feed the Earth's inhabitants? The answer depends on the definition of "enough." The food supply available in 1990 could support 6 billion people on a basic, primarily vegetarian, diet of 2,350 calories per person per day. Adding animal products to compose 10 percent of the caloric intake, equivalent to a Latin American diet, would result in feeding only 4 billion people. With a diet that resembles that of much of the developed world, containing 30 percent animal products, only 2.5 billion people, less than half of the world's population in 1990 would be fed.[24]

Extinction of Plant and Animal Species

Throughout history, human societies have domesticated wild animal and plant species for their own use. Agricultural activities continue with this tradition, and technological advances have recently made genetic engineering possible, creating another use for wild animals and plants. This technology, as well as earlier ones, however, depends on a wide variety of species. One of the most significant threats to the Earth's environment is that to biodiversity. Until industrialization, the human population had little effect on nature's extinction rate, estimated at 90 species per century. With growing numbers of people, and their increasing consumption patterns, the extinction rate has grown markedly. Deforestation is a major threat to biodiversity, as 50 to 90 percent of all animal and plant species live in tropical moist forests. Approximately two-thirds of the wildlife habitats in Southeast Asia and sub-Saharan Africa have been destroyed. If present deforestation trends continue, 12 percent of all bird species and 15 percent of all plant species will be lost by the year 2000. Because island species have particularly fragile ecosystems, three-fourths of all recently extinct mammal and bird species lived on islands.[25]

PROSPECTS FOR HUMAN SURVIVAL AND QUALITY OF LIFE

Although demographers may disagree on how fast the world's population will grow and when the human population will reach its peak, almost all of them would agree that the world's population will probably be considerably more dense in coming years than it has been in the past. It is likely that people living in what are now developing countries will demand access to the higher living standards that people in developed countries currently enjoy. If the population grows to such an extent that a high living standard is not possible for all, and if the current level of inequality becomes unacceptable, then living standards all over the world will have to change as one of the consequences of life in a more crowded world.

One possible change in living standards is in diet. The high-calorie, high-fat diets of many who live in developed societies may be extremely expensive or even unavailable in future years. Another resource that may be controlled more stringently is energy, particularly fossil fuels, not only because we may run out of them, but also because their use results in intolerable levels of pollution. As populations increase, the efficiency with which water is used and reused will have to increase, affecting both individual consumers and commercial plants. As the number of large cities grow, air pollution will tend to become much more intense. Each city will find that more and more of its air has been polluted from emissions rising over other cities. As a result, further national and international controls over air and water pollution will become necessary.

A direct result of crowding will be that the amount of space per capita will decrease. Even in the United States, where general living space is still ample, crowding will have immediate consequences, although even now the country suffers from overcrowding in its places of prime scenic and historic interest. In recent years, the number of visits to the national park system approached 300 million a year—approximately 30 times the annual number of visitors in the 1930s.[26] This problem may be dealt with in the future by prohibiting automobiles in some or all places, limiting human access, and perhaps even prohibiting people from visiting certain fragile parts of the national park system.

Environmental survival in a more crowded world will depend on our ability to make changes continually as the environment demands. Because the effects of human life on the environment may not appear for decades, we must rely on computer simulations to project the outcomes of alternative scenarios, and we must be willing to accept changes in our life-styles for the benefit of future generations.

NOTES

1. Ehrlich, Paul R., and Anne H. Ehrlich, *The Population Explosion* (New York: Simon and Schuster, 1990), pp. 26–30.

2. French, Hilary F., "Clearing the Air," in *State of the World 1990: A Worldwatch Institute Report on Progress Toward a Sustainable Society* (New York: W. W. Norton & Company, 1990), pp. 98–118.
3. Magder, Richard, with Thomas Merrick, "America in the 21st Century: Environmental Concerns" (Washington, DC: Population Reference Bureau, February 1990).
4. Ibid.
5. Harrison, G. A. et al., *Human Biology* (Oxford: Oxford University Press, 1977), pp. 408–413; and Bryant, Carol A., et al., *The Cultural Feast* (St. Paul: West Publishing Co., 1985), pp. 21–32.
6. Bryant et al., *The Cultural Feast*, pp. 54–58.
7. Ehrlich and Ehrlich, *The Population Explosion*, p. 67.
8. World Resources Institute, with the International Institute for Environment and Development, in collaboration with the United Nations Environment Programme, *World Resources 1988–89* (New York: Basic Books, 1989), pp. 53–54.
9. Ehrlich and Ehrlich, *The Population Explosion*, pp. 41, 67.
10. Flavin, Christopher, "Slowing Global Warming," in *State of the World 1990*, pp. 17–38.
11. French, Hilary F., "Clearing the Air," in *State of the World 1990*, pp. 98–118.
12. Flavin, Christopher, "Reassessing Nuclear Power," in *State of the World 1987* (New York: W. W. Norton & Company, 1987), pp. 57–80.
13. Magder with Merrick, "America in the 21st Century."
14. World Resources Institute, *World Resources 1988–89*, pp. 70–71.
15. Ibid.
16. Ibid., pp. 10–11; and Curtis Skinner, "Population Myth and the Third World," *Social Policy*, 19 (Summer 1988), 57–62.
17. Ibid.
18. Ibid.
19. World Resources Institute, *World Resources 1988–89*, pp. 109-111.
20. *The Economist*, May 12, 1990, p. 9.
21. Schneider, Stephen H., "The Changing Climate," *Scientific American*, 261, 3 (September 1989), 70–79.
22. Brown, Lester R., and John E. Young, "Feeding the World in the Nineties," in *State of the World 1990*, pp. 59–78; and Lester R. Brown, "Global Ecology at the Brink," interview in *Challenge* (March–April 1989), pp. 14–22.
23. Goliber, Thomas J., "Africa's Expanding Population: Old Problems, New Policies," *Population Bulletin*, 44, 3 (Washington, DC: Population Reference Bureau, November 1989).
24. World Resources Institute, *World Resources 1988–89*, p. 53.
25. Ibid., pp. 5, 89–93.
26. U.S. Bureau of the Census, *Statistical Abstract of the United States 1990* (Washington, DC: U.S. Government Printing Office), p. 222.

CHAPTER 4
MORTALITY

MEASUREMENT OF MORTALITY

The *crude death rate*, perhaps the most commonly used measure of mortality, can be defined as the ratio of the number of deaths that occur within a given population during a specified year to the size of that population at midyear. Frequently, however, the crude death rate does not provide a very accurate indicator of mortality conditions, since the age structure affects its measurement. A young population will have a lower crude death rate than an older population if the death rates at each age in the two populations are identical. Sometimes a younger population will have a lower crude death rate even if its age-specific death rates are higher than those of the older population.

An exact comparison of mortality in two different populations can be made by a separate presentation of the death rates in each age–sex group of each population. This method is illustrated in Table 4–1, which presents male age-specific death rates for the United States and for Mexico in 1985. Table 4–1 shows clearly that at each age below age 60, mortality is higher for males in Mexico than for males in the United States. After age 60, mortality for males is higher in the United States than in Mexico. Because Mexico has a younger population, its 1985 crude death rate was lower than the U.S. male crude death rate. The table also demonstrates the very great differences in mortality by age within each of these two populations. For both nations, the death rates by age form roughly a U-shaped distribution. Death rates are relatively high among infants, decline rapidly in early childhood, reach their minimum around ages 10 to 14, and then rise gradually but steadily through the older ages.

Life tables provide the most complete picture of mortality in a given population. Two types of life tables can be constructed. The most common is the

Table 4–1.   Male Age-Specific Deaths for the United States and for Mexico, 1985 (per 1,000 population)

AGE	UNITED STATES	MEXICO
All ages	9.5	5.9
0–4	3.0	8.4
5–9	0.3	0.7
10–14	0.3	0.7
15–19	1.1	1.4
20–24	1.6	2.4
25–29	1.7	3.0
30–34	1.9	3.3
35–39	2.4	4.7
40–44	3.3	5.9
45–49	5.1	7.8
50–54	8.4	10.1
55–59	13.4	14.2
60–64	20.6	19.5
65–69	30.6	28.1
70–74	47.5	41.4
75–79	71.4	65.2
80 & over	139.5	163.8

Sources: Death rates for Mexico from United Nations, 1988 Demographic Yearbook (New York: United Nations, 1990), pp. 476–477, copyright, United Nations (1990), reproduced by permission; U.S. Death Rates from National Center for Health Statistics, Vital Statistics of the United States, 1985, vol 2 Mortality, part A (Washington, DC: Public Health Service, 1988), section 1, pp. 10–11; and calculated from National Center for Health Statistics, Vital Statistics of the United States, 1985, vol 2, Mortality, part A (Washington, DC: Public Health Service, 1988), section 1, pp. 244–245, and U.S. Bureau of the Census, Current Population Reports, Series P-25, no. 1000, Estimates of the Population of the United States, by Age, Sex, and Race: 1980–1986 (Washington, DC: U.S. Government Printing Office, 1987).

period life table, which summarizes the age-specific mortality conditions of a given year. The second type, called the cohort, or generation, life table, summarizes the age-specific mortality experience of a given birth cohort (a group of persons born at the same time) for its lifetime, and thus extends over many calendar years. Usually life tables are computed separately for males and females, as well as for different racial and ethnic groups.

Both types of life tables assume an artificial cohort of fixed size at birth—usually 100,000—and then "expose" those individuals to the age-specific mortality rates of the "real" population. The life table procedure generates the following information for each year of age: (1) the probability of death during the year for those persons entering an exact age x: q_x; (2) the number of deaths occurring between exact age x and exact age x + 1: d_x; (3) the number of survivors to exact age x: l_x; (4) the number of years of life lived by the cohort between exact age x and age x + 1: L_x; (5) the total years of life lived by the cohort from age x to the end

Table 4–2. Abridged Life Table for the Female Population: United States, 1987

AGE INTERVAL	PROPORTION DYING	OF 100,000 BORN ALIVE		STATIONARY POPULATION		AVERAGE REMAINING LIFETIME
PERIOD OF LIFE BETWEEN TWO EXACT AGES STATED IN YEARS, RACE, AND SEX	PROPORTION OF PERSONS ALIVE AT BEGINNING OF AGE INTERVAL DYING DURING INTERVAL	NUMBER LIVING AT BEGINNING OF AGE INTERVAL	NUMBER DYING DURING AGE INTERVAL	IN THE AGE INTERVAL	IN THIS AND ALL SUBSEQUENT AGE INTERVALS	AVERAGE NUMBER OF YEARS OF LIFE REMAINING AT BEGINNING OF AGE INTERVAL
(1) x to $x + n$	(2) nqx	(3) lx	(4) ndx	(5) nLx	(6) Tx	(7) $e\overset{o}{x}$
0–1	.0090	100,000	896	99,236	7,836,924	78.4
1–5	.0018	99,104	177	395,993	7,737,688	78.1
5–10	.0010	98,927	96	494,374	7,341,695	74.2
10–15	.0009	98,831	91	493,958	6,847,321	69.3
15–20	.0024	98,740	237	493,145	6,353,363	64.3
20–25	.0027	98,503	271	491,850	5,860,218	59.5
25–30	.0032	98,232	317	490,384	5,368,368	54.6
30–35	.0042	97,915	409	488,600	4,877,984	49.8
35–40	.0058	97,506	562	486,224	4,389,384	45.0
40–45	.0084	96,944	810	482,845	3,903,160	40.3
45–50	.0137	96,134	1,319	477,612	3,420,315	35.6
50–55	.0224	94,815	2,122	469,099	2,942,703	31.0
55–60	.0342	92,693	3,174	455,998	2,473,604	26.7
60–65	.0540	89,519	4,831	436,220	2,017,606	22.5
65–70	.0796	84,688	6,737	407,479	1,581,386	18.7
70–75	.1213	77,951	9,458	367,324	1,173,907	15.1
75–80	.1840	68,493	12,604	312,442	806,583	11.8
80–85	.2937	55,889	16,416	239,551	494,141	8.8
85 and over	1.0000	39,473	39,473	254,590	254,590	6.4

Source: National Center for Health Statistics, Vital Statistics of the United States, 1987, vol. 2, Mortality, Part A (Washington, DC: Public Health Service, 1990), section 6, p. 6.

of the human lifespan: T_x; and (6) the mean number of years of life remaining from age x to the end of the life span: $e°_x$.

A variant of the complete life table, which provides mortality data for each single year of age, is the *abridged* life table, which provides data for persons in particular age groups, usually of 5-year intervals. An abridged life table for U.S. females in 1989 is presented in Table 4–2. In this table the prefix n refers to the number of years in the age interval. Thus $_nL_x$ denotes the number of years life lived between age x and age x+n.

Perhaps the most commonly used datum from the life table is the *average* or *mean expectation of life at birth*, $e°_0$. A principal advantage of the mean expectation of life at birth as a summary measure of mortality is that, unlike the crude death rate, it is not affected by the age structure of the population. It is important to distinguish *life expectancy* from *life span*. Whereas the former is an average and reflects actual mortality conditions, the latter is the theoretical maximum number of years that an individual can live under optimal conditions. For humans, life span is estimated to be on the order of 100 years, although reliable evidence has shown humans living just past 120 years. One working definition of life span is the age at which less than 0.1 percent of the population survives.[1] Life expectancy can fluctuate with mortality rates, but life span is considered to be more stable over time both for humans and other animal species.

Two additional summary measures of mortality are also free of distortion due to differences in age composition. One of these is the *age-standardized*, or *age-adjusted, death rate*. This is obtained by computing for each age group the product of its death rate and a fraction equal to the proportion belonging to that particular age group in a "standard" population and then summing these products over every age group. Mortality in various populations may be easily compared when the same standard population is used to "weight" the age-specific mortality rates in each population. Another frequently used measure of mortality is the *standard mortality ratio*, which equals 100 times the ratio of the actual crude death rate in a population to the rate that would have been expected if for each age group in the actual population the death rate were identical to that in some "standard" population. Mortality in various populations can again be easily compared when standard mortality ratios are computed for several populations, in every case using the same set of rates as the standard in constructing the "expected" death rate.

MORTALITY DETERMINANTS

Mortality is a consequence both of *morbidity* (sickness) and of the *case-fatality* rate (the proportion of sick persons who die). *Curative measures*, primarily through medical institutions and their practitioners, treat morbidity after it occurs and have been available in varying degrees of effectiveness throughout human history. Whereas curative measures attempt to reduce case-fatality rates, *preventive measures* focus on reducing both morbidity and case fatality. Some of the significant preventive measures include providing an adequate level of nutrition and exercise, improving public health conditions, implementing immunization programs, and eliminating unhealthy behaviors (such as smoking).

Although malnutrition is not usually a primary cause of death, it is responsible for making people more susceptible to acquiring infectious diseases. Furthermore, malnourished persons have a more difficult time recovering from sickness. Malnutrition contributes at least in part to approximately one-third of the childhood deaths around the world each year.[2] Diet is not just an issue for persons in developing countries. Numerous studies dating from the 1940s have linked excess dietary fat with coronary heart disease in Western nations. While some populations consuming relatively large levels of animal fat may have lower levels of coronary heart disease than do populations consuming less dietary fat, the evidence is overwhelming that certain individuals who consume high-fat diets may increase their risk of coronary heart disease.[3]

Several developments in the nineteenth and twentieth centuries effected improvements in public health conditions in both Europe and the United States. Even earlier, governments enforced the quarantine of infected persons to prevent further spread of disease, although quarantines are effective only if the disease is spread through casual contact.[4] Two other major public health measures are adequate disposal of sewage and a pure water supply. In the opinion of one expert, these two measures have done more for the health of human beings than any other hygienic measures.[5]

Edwin Chadwick, an English barrister, argued the causal connection between sanitary care and disease and urged that each local unit of government appoint a physician as a salaried health officer. The Public Health Act of 1848, passed largely through Chadwick's efforts, provided, for the first time, a statutory authority for such health officers.[6] An additional impetus for improving water supplies emerged when John Snow, a London physician, proved that the incidence of cholera during the epidemic of 1848 was especially high in those areas of the city where the drinking water was of lowest quality. A similar discovery with respect to typhoid fever was soon made by another English physician, William Budd.[7]

In addition to disposing of sewage and providing a clean water supply, other public health interventions that have helped to reduce mortality include spraying insecticides to kill malaria-carrying mosquitoes, developing fire departments and fire-safety building codes, and improving transportation systems. Better transportation improves health indirectly, by improving the delivery of food and medical supplies, and thus makes both preventive and curative measures more effective.

Immunization against specific infectious diseases began with Edward Jenner's discovery in 1771 that smallpox could be prevented by injection of material obtained from persons infected with the milder disease of cowpox. In the latter half of the nineteenth century, the bacteriological and viral theory of disease was developed by Louis Pasteur, Robert Koch, and others. Pasteur dramatically proved that immunization against certain diseases could be accomplished by inoculation with a live but attenuated organism when he developed first his famous vaccine that saved thousands of European sheep and cattle from the scourge of anthrax, and then the celebrated vaccine that prevents rabies from developing in human beings. Since the late nineteenth century, vaccines have been developed for many infectious diseases.[8] Mass immunization has played a major role in making death from infectious disease uncommon in developed nations, and has brought about a substantial decline in mortality from such diseases in the less developed nations. That humans rely so extensively on immunizations and perhaps even take them for granted was made poignant by the lack of a vaccine for human immunodeficiency virus (HIV), which leads to acquired immune deficiency syndrome (AIDS).

Ordinary changes in life-style that do not require medical technology, particularly those that eliminate unhealthy behaviors, can prevent both infectious and degenerative diseases. Improvements in personal hygiene—bathing, hand washing, laundering, and maintaining clean living quarters—contributed to the early decline in mortality in Western nations. Her experience during the Crimean War (1854–1856) led Florence Nightingale to collect and analyze statistics on preventable deaths among soldiers and then use these data to argue for improved sanitary conditions in hospital barracks.[9] In the twentieth century, preventive health measures have increasingly included educating the public about the dangers of cigarette smoking and the use of alcohol and other addictive drugs. Another life-style change that has been shown to reduce cardiovascular disease is a program of regular, moderate exercise to counteract the sedentary way of life in a modern society.

The technology of curative medicine has also made great advances since the middle of the nineteenth century. One of the most important, made around 1865, was Joseph Lister's development of antisepsis (antiseptic methods), which greatly reduced the risk of infection during and after surgery.[10] Another major advance, begun in 1928, was the development of antibiotics, which was initiated by Alexander Fleming's discovery that the mold *penicillium notatum* could kill staphylococci.[11] Widespread use of antibiotics during and after World War II led to substantial reductions in deaths as a result of wounds and of many diseases, such as tuberulosis, bubonic plague, typhoid, and typhus, although these diseases still claim many lives, particularly in the developing world.

More recently, medical technology has developed procedures and drugs that alter the course of many degenerative diseases. Medications for hypertension, diabetes, and cardiac conditions have prolonged many lives, as have kidney dialysis, organ transplants, angioplasty, and open heart surgery. The prognosis for many forms of cancer has improved dramatically over the recent decades as advances have been made in the use of surgery, chemotherapy, and radiation.

MORTALITY TRENDS

Developed Countries

Industrialization and the concomitant development of effective preventive and curative measures defined the mortality trends for what are now the developed countries of the world. As life expectancy rose, degenerative diseases increasingly overtook infectious diseases as the leading causes of death. Omran devised a theory of epidemiological transition to describe and explain historical mortality trends. The first stage, *the age of pestilence and famine*, is one of high deaths rates on average, with extremely high peaks corresponding to periodic epidemics. Infants and children were particularly susceptible to contracting and dying from infectious and parasitic diseases. Also at this time, maternal mortality (deaths during pregnancy, childbirth, and immediately following childbirth) was also quite high. Life expectancy for this period was under 40 years.[12]

As societal reforms improved health conditions, the second stage, *the age of receding pandemics*, emerged, improving survival rates for infants, children, and women of childbearing age. The high peaks in mortality rates flattened as proportionally fewer people developed infectious diseases and as those who did become ill were more likely to regain their health. Life expectancy rose to at least 50 during this period.[13]

The third stage that Omran outlined was *the age of degenerative disease*. He saw this stage as a final one, where life expectancy reached a plateau of approximately 70 years and the predominant causes of death were degenerative diseases. At the time Omran published his theory, it did indeed appear that humanity had reached the biological limits to life expectancy.[14] However, medical technology and life-style changes have brought about significant reductions in mortality from such causes as cancer and cardiovascular disease, so that Oshansky and Ault argued for a fourth stage, *the age of delayed degenerative disease*. While the transitions to the second and third stages were brought on by changes in the causes of death, the shift to the fourth stage involves changing the age pattern of degenerative-disease mortality. Society has not eliminated degenerative diseases (as has happened for many infectious diseases), but has instead allowed individuals to live longer, dying at later ages.[15]

The epidemiological transition model does indeed fit the experience of northern and western Europe, North America, Australia, and New Zealand. As the age of pestilence and famine was ending in these areas, life expectancy averaged around 40 years, the highest attained in human history, except for small elite populations. By 1900, the average life expectancy reached 50 years, and by 1950 it was approaching 70 years. Not all European countries experienced their mortality declines this early. In many parts of southern and eastern Europe, life expectancy had not reached 40 years by 1900, although in the first few decades of the twentieth century, mortality rates in these places plummeted to the levels of those in the rest of the developed world. Similar rapid mortality declines took place in East Asia (most notably Japan) and in temperate South America (Argentina) during the middle of the twentieth century.[16]

By the late 1980s, life expectancy at birth reached an average of 74 years in the more developed countries, ranging from 69 years to 77 years. The most favorable mortality conditions were found in Japan, followed by northern European countries. Among the developed nations, southern and eastern European countries (including the Soviet Union) had the lowest life expectancies. The most significant mortality declines took place at either end of the life span.[17]

Infant mortality fell dramatically during the late 1970s and 1980s, due to proportionately fewer high-risk pregnancies and improved medical technology that has allowed fragile infants, particularly those weighing less than 5.5 pounds, to survive. The increased acceptance of contraception has reduced the incidence of high-risk pregnancies, particularly among older women and women with serious health conditions. Medical advances in the 1970s and 1980s made it possible to identify high-risk pregnancies and either terminate them or intervene medically in order to increase the likelihood that the newborn infant would be healthy.[18]

The fourth stage of the epidemiological transition, delaying degenerative diseases, resulted in large, unanticipated declines in old-age mortality. Between 1968 and 1977, U.S. mortality rates for ages 85 and above declined faster than those for any other age group except for infants.[19] Up through 1984, the U.S. Census Bureau's population projections severely underestimated the size of the older population because estimates of mortality declines in these ages were too conservative. Since then, the Census Bureau has included more than one set of mortality assumptions in order to estimate a range of possibilities.[20]

Recognizing a fourth stage of the epidemiological transition leads us to ask two questions. First, is it possible for life expectancy to increase significantly more? And second, are people living longer and healthier lives, or are the added years of life spent in disability? Researchers have presented diverging answers to both questions. Some speculate that it may be possible for life expectancy to approach the human life span of 100 years, while others suggest that pushing life expectancy past 85 years is impossible without practically eliminating deaths due to the major degenerative diseases.[21] The debate over whether living longer means living with sustained health revolves around definitions of disability and morbidity. In the United States between 1970 and 1980, the added years of life expectancy consisted primarily of years of long-term disability, although below age 85, most of the added years of life were not spent bedridden, even though individuals may report themselves to be otherwise disabled.[22]

There is also a possibility that mortality can increase even after reaching extremely low levels. Certain population subgroups in developed countries have already experienced increasing mortality, most notably young adult males in the United States (as a result of AIDS deaths). For an entire population, however, once mortality begins to decline, it does not usually reverse. An important exception to this generalization occurred in the Soviet Union between 1964 and 1982, when adult male mortality rose considerably, with overall life expectancy declining from 66 years to 62 years. Possible explanations for this decline are first, worsening health conditions, particularly increased smoking and alcohol consumption, poor diet, and substandard health care; second, an improvement in the reporting of deaths; and third, increased mortality among cohorts born during World War II, when living conditions were especially harsh and resulted in lifelong health problems. While the latter two situations indeed occurred, they cannot account for a majority of the increase in mortality. Links between rising mortality and specific changes in Soviet healthcare policy or health behavior have been difficult to prove conclusively.[23]

Developing Countries

Even though mortality improvements began in the early part of the twentieth century in some developing countries, after World War II mortality plummeted at unprecedented rates, sweeping many countries into a demographic transition and setting the stage for high rates of population growth. Life expectancy gains of 20 to 30 years took place over a similar period of time in, for example, Trinidad, Sri Lanka, and Taiwan. Equivalent gains in the western developed countries required 50 to 100 years.[24]

Just as mortality did not decline uniformly in developed countries, tremendous variation has characterized the mortality declines among the developing world. Of all developing regions, East Asia led the way in mortality declines, and by the end of the 1980s, many of these countries had life expectancies within the range of those found in the so-called developed world. Southeast Asia has lagged behind East Asia, while many western Asian countries (also known as the Middle East) have achieved relatively high life expectancies (75 years in Israel and Cyprus). During most of the twentieth century, mortality levels in South Asia were the worst on the continent. In India there were rapid improvements in the late 1970s after a period of little progress in the early 1970s.[25]

Mortality declines in Latin America have also been fairly diverse, with the largest gains in parts of the Caribbean and in temperate South America. Countries in tropical South America have reached mortality levels somewhat more favorable than those in South Asia.[26]

Countries in Africa began their mortality transition after most of Asia and Latin America. By the mid 1970s, life expectancy at birth was less than 40 years for three countries (Gambia, Sierra Leone, and Malawi), and little progress has occurred since then. North Africa and South Africa have made the greatest progress in reducing mortality, while West Africa is the furthest behind in the mortality transition.[27] In the late 1970s, HIV, the virus responsible for AIDS, began spreading among the heterosexual population in central, eastern, and southern Africa. In some urban areas, as much as one-fourth of the sexually active population was infected by the end of the 1980s. AIDS is projected to reduce the size of the 0-to-4 population in a typical sub-Saharan African country by more than 25 percent by 1997 and is expected to eliminate approximately one-half of the potential growth of the 25-to-59-year age group.[28]

While medical technology was not responsible for the large part of the mortality decline in the developed world, it has been instrumental in lowering mortality in developing countries, although it has not necessarily been in the hands of modern medical personnel like physicians, nurses, and pharmacists. In many rural areas of South Asia and Africa, persons trained in their society's traditional medical techniques, as well as completely untrained persons, dispense medical knowledge and drugs through informal networks and provide referral services to the formal health sector as well.[29]

MORTALITY DIFFERENTIALS

Apart from age, the most important demographic variable is sex, and in every society, males and females face different mortality risks, for both biological and social reasons. Moreover, sex differences in mortality show consistent patterns both historically and regionally, with female life expectancy showing more variation than male life expectancy. Generally speaking, women live longer than men, except in a few societies in South Asia and the Middle East, although even there, the male advantage vanishes after the childbearing years. In 1988, male life expectancy was 2.3 years higher than female life expectancy for Bangladesh, whereas in Thailand, females lived an average of 6.5 years more than males. In most South Asian and Middle Eastern countries, male children receive preferential nutrition and health care, and maternal mortality is especially high.[30] Societies with lower mortality tend to experience a wider female advantage, although this effect appears to have taken place primarily after World War II, reflecting behavioral differences between men and women, and may not be an essential correlate of declining mortality.[31]

In the United States, the male disadvantage in life expectancy jumped from 3.5 years in 1930 to 6.8 years in 1988. The increasing male disadvantage in mortality in the United States and other developed countries appears to stem primarily from the greater propensity of men to smoke cigarettes in the first half of the twentieth century, and has resulted in higher levels of lung cancer and heart disease for men. To a greater extent than women, men have also tended to adopt other riskier behaviors, such as heavy alcohol use and reckless driving, which has increased their mortality disadvantage. Men also tend to work in occupations that place them at a higher risk of fatal accidents on the job and greater exposure to toxic substances that can affect their health over the longer term. There does not seem to be any reliable evidence that increased labor force participation for women will lessen their mortality advantage. Rather, any future reduction in the mortality sex differential will likely reflect increased cigarette smoking among women.[32]

Even though male mortality exceeds female mortality, women tend to be less healthy than men. They report more illnesses and visit physicians more frequently than do men. One reason could be that women are more likely than men to seek medical help which could lead to their lower mortality rates. Women also tend to suffer more from nonfatal chronic diseases, which require ongoing medical attention, whereas men have a higher incidence of fatal diseases.[33]

In most developed countries, the AIDS epidemic has affected male mortality in the 20-to-49 age group, because homosexual and bisexual men and male intravenous drug users constitute the primary infected population.[34] The extent to which HIV infections spread to other groups—for example, the female partners of bisexual men and male intravenous drug users—will shape the mortality trends of other age groups as well.

Another important mortality differential is social class. Throughout most of human history, persons of higher social position have enjoyed better food and living conditions, which translate to better health and lower mortality. With the advent of modern medicine, socioeconomic differences in mortality increased, as access to modern health care has not been uniform in most societies. In developing societies, mothers with more education are more likely to adopt regular hygiene habits, not because such habits improve health *per se*, but because they believe that well-educated women use these kinds of practices in conducting their households. In ·addition, mothers with more education tend to have more autonomy and resources for providing their children with sufficient nutrition and medical care, and thus they experience lower levels of infant and child mortality.[35]

Increasing socioeconomic mortality differentials were observed in the United States between 1940 and 1970, a reversal of earlier patterns of convergence. As degenerative diseases become a larger factor in mortality, knowledge and practice of low-risk life-styles, along with access to health care, become increasingly important, and in the United States, the middle and upper classes have benefited more than the lower classes. Overall life expectancy in the United States could be raised more by eliminating socioeconomic differences than by eliminating cancer deaths, demonstrating that technology is not the complete answer to reducing mortality.[36]

For the United States, the effect of social class manifests itself in the differential mortality of whites and African-Americans. While infant mortality declined markedly between 1960 and 1989 (from 26.0 to 9.7 deaths per 1,000 live births overall), significant differences persist between white and African-American rates. In 1987, the infant mortality rate for whites was 8.6, whereas for African-Americans it was 17.9—more than twice as high. The single best determinant of infant mortality is low birth weight (less than 2,500 grams, or about 5.5 pounds), and while the likelihood of having a low-birth-weight infant declined for white mothers between 1960 and 1980, it increased for African-American mothers. Even controlling for a large number of risk factors associated with both the infant and the mother, African-American infants still had significantly higher death rates than white infants. One possible reason is that African-American women and infants often do not receive adequate prenatal or postnatal care.[37]

The mortality disadvantage of African-Americans continues throughout life, although the gap in mortality rates does lessen with age, and there is evidence for a "cross-over" effect at the oldest ages; that is, among the very old, African-Americans may have lower mortality rates than whites. Overall, however, African-American life expectancy at birth was 69.7 years, 6.2 years less than that of whites in 1989.[38] In Harlem, a section of New York City where 96 percent of the population is African-American, 1980 mortality rates for men under age 65 were higher than those in Bangladesh. Similar differentials have been shown for racial minority populations in other inner-city neighborhoods.[39] Unfortunately, racial differences in life expectancy, which had declined until the mid 1980s, began to increase again as white mortality rates improved faster than African-American mortality rates.[40] It is possible that African-American mortality rates will increase, primarily because of AIDS, but also because of the worsening conditions of African-American neighborhoods and health care for persons in these communities.

Another important determinant of health and mortality for adults in industrialized countries is marital status. In contrast to single, divorced, and widowed persons, married persons experience lower levels of morbidity and mortality. Two theories could account for this finding. One argues that marriage protects individuals, through social, economic, and psychological factors, from disease. The second theory argues that marriage selects for the healthier individuals in a population. With cross-sectional data, it is difficult to know whether marriage is the cause or the result of healthy behavior. Marital status also interacts with gender, as the health benefits of marriage are greater for men than for women. Unmarried men between the ages of 20 and 65 living in developed countries have twice the mortality rates, on average, of unmarried women.[41] Extending the findings regarding marital status more generally, persons with a dearth of (high-quality) social relationships face increased mortality risks.[42]

SOCIAL EFFECTS OF MORTALITY DECLINE

It is possible that the dramatic decline in mortality since the end of the nineteenth century has evoked more changes in social structure than any other single development of the period. Contemporary citizens of developed societies rarely encounter death, except among the aged and extremely disadvantaged socioeconomic groups. This situation contrasts greatly to that which prevailed in these nations in former times. To illustrate how different the past situation was in our own country, let us note some of the bereavements suffered by three presidents of the United States and their families. George Washington's father died when George was only 11 years old. Before her marriage to George, Martha Custis Washington was a 26-year-old widow. She had already borne four children, two of whom had died in infancy; and of her two surviving children, one died at age 17 and the other in early adulthood. Thomas Jefferson lost his father when he was only 14 years old. His wife, Martha, had also been previously widowed when she married Tom at the age of 23, and she herself died only 11 years later. Of the six children that Martha and Tom bore, only two lived to maturity. Abraham Lincoln's mother died when she was 35 and he was 9. She had three children; one son died in infancy, and the daughter died in her early 20s. Of the four children born to Abraham and Mary Todd Lincoln, only one survived to maturity.[43] Clearly these lives, often among those most privileged in U.S. society, endured many more bereavements than is typical today.

A seemingly direct consequence of the decline in the frequency of mourning is the decline in the associated norms of bereavement. At the beginning of the twentieth century, the bereaved and those around them observed strict rules of etiquette. With longer lives becoming a near certainty, the norms regarding bereavement are less clear and well known, with the result that individuals try to deny the very existence of the bereavement. The lack of bereavement ritual and the frequent attempt to act as if the death had not occurred combine to encumber the healing process and prolong the period of mourning.[44]

One of the important patterns of modernization is secularization, or the decline in the influence of religion. In premodern societies, individuals turned to religious practitioners to explain the mysteries of life, and one of the most salient of these was health or its inverse, illness. As humans have been able to control the forces of mortality, individuals increasingly rely on health professionals rather than religious leaders to solve health problems, one example of secularization in a modern society.[45]

Economic institutions are beginning to adjust to the changes in mortality, although they still lag behind increasing years of life expectancy. Around 1930, just before passage of the Social Security Act, the average 60-year-old white man could expect to live another 14.7 years, and 60-year-old white women another 16.1 years. By 1986, these figures had increased to 18.2 years and 22.6 years, respectively.[46] While life expectancy rose during this period, labor force participation of older persons, particularly men, declined as older persons became more likely to retire and entered retirement at earlier ages.[47] As persons in the earlier years of old age have acquired better health, logically speaking, retirement ages should be increasing rather than decreasing. With a growing population in the prime working-age years, however, the United States has been able to afford to have large numbers of older persons out of the labor force. As the baby-boom generation reaches older ages during the twenty-first century, the economy may need to have larger proportions of older persons in the labor force.

Of all social institutions, the one affected most by mortality declines is the family. First, as children are more likely to survive, parents tend to become more emotionally attached to them, thus changing the nature of parent–child relations. With declines in adult mortality, children are less likely to experience the death of one or two parents, making social institutions like orphanages somewhat obsolete, and changing the role of godparents, for example, from that of caretakers of orphans to that of mentors assisting the parents. As mortality has declined into the older ages, children are more likely to have living grandparents, and to spend more years with them. Four- or five-generation families have also become a relatively common, rather than rare occurrence. One explanation for the rising divorce rate is that declining mortality has made it possible for marriages to last several decades before being broken by death. Under the mortality conditions operating in 1900, two-thirds of all marriages would end within 40 years by the death of one spouse. By 1976, without divorce, only about one-third of marriages would end within 40 years. Because female mortality has declined faster than male mortality, women experience an extended period of widowhood at the end of their lives. Decreased mortality at older ages has led middle-aged children to spend more adult years with living parents. In 1980, women who survived to age 15 could expect to spend twice as many years with one or more parents alive as could women in 1800. Perhaps the most significant effect of declining mortality is its effect on fertility. As infant and child mortality decline, parents are able to have fewer children, as they no longer need to have additional children for "insurance purposes" to ensure the survival of the number they want. The mechanisms for both instigating and continuing a fertility decline will be discussed in the following chapter.[48]

NOTES

1. Shryock, Henry S., Jacob S. Siegal, et al., *The Methods and Materials of Demography*, condensed ed., by Edward G. Stockwell (New York: Academic Press, 1976), p. 253.
2. The World Resources Institute and the International Institute for Environment and Development, in collaboration with The United Nations Environment Programme, *World Resources 1988–89* (New York: Basic Books, Inc. 1990), p. 26.
3. Smil, Vaclav, "Coronary Heart Disease, Diet, and Western Mortality," *Population and Development Review*, 15, 3 (September 1989), 399–424.
4. This is one reason that quarantines for AIDS patients have had no support in the medical community. William H. McNeil, in *Plagues and Peoples* (New York: Anchor Press, Doubleday, 1976), states that quarantines of persons with the plague in fourteenth-century Europe were not effective because that disease was spread by rats, not by human contact.
5. Brockington, C. Fraser, *Public Health in the Nineteenth Century* (Edinburgh: E. & S. Livingstone, 1965), p. v.
6. Ibid., pp. 136–63.
7. Wilcocks, Charles, *Medical Advance, Public Health and Social Evolution* (Oxford: Pergamon Press, 1965), pp. 105–106.
8. Ibid., pp. 118–134.
9. Cohen, I. Bernard, "Florence Nightingale," *Scientific American*, 250, 3 (March 1984), pp. 128–137.
10. Wilcocks, *Medical Advance*, pp. 115–17.
11. Ibid., pp. 201–209.
12. Omran, Abdel, "The Epidemiological Transition: A Theory of the Epidemiology of Population Change," *Milbank Memorial Fund Quarterly*, 49, 4, pt. 1 (October 1971), 509–538.
13. Ibid.
14. Ibid.
15. Olshansky, S. Jay, and A. Brian Ault, "The Fourth Stage of the Epidemiologic Transition: The Age of Delayed Degenerative Diseases," *The Milbank Memorial Fund Quarterly*, 64, 3 (July 1986), pp. 355–391.
16. United Nations, Department of Economic and Social Affairs, *The Determinants and Consequences of Population Trends: New Summary of Findings on Interaction of Demographic, Economic and Social Factors*, vol. 1, Population Studies, no. 50 (New York: United Nations, 1973), pp. 110–113.
17. United Nations, Department of International Economic and Social Affairs, *World Population: Trends and Policies, 1987 Monitoring Report* (New York: United Nations, 1988), pp. 134–136.
18. United Nations, *World Population*, p. 141.
19. Crimmins, Eileen M., "The Changing Pattern of American Mortality Decline, 1940–77, and Its Implications for the Future," *Population and Development Review*, 7, 2 (June 1981), 229–253.
20. Serow, William J., David F. Sly, and J. Michael Wrigley, *Population Aging in the United States* (New York: Greenwood Press, 1990), p. 35.
21. Manton, Kenneth, Max Woodbury, and Eric Stallard, "Forecasts of the Theoretical Limits to Human Life Expectancy," in *Aging and Dying: The Biological Foundations of Human Longevity*, ed. Sheila Johansson (Berkeley: University of California Press, 1990), show that life expectancy could exceed 99 years, whereas Olshansky, S. Jay, B.

A. Carnes, and C. Cassel, "In Search of Methuselah: Estimating the Upper Limits to Human Longevity," *Science* 250 (Nov. 2, 1990), pp. 634–640, argue the unlikelihood of life expectancy exceeding 85 years.

22. Crimmins, Eileen M., Yashuiko Saito, and Dominique Ingegneri, "Changes in Life Expectancy and Disability-Free Life Expectancy in the United States," *Population and Development Review*, 15, 2 (June 1989), pp. 235–267.

23. Anderson, Barbara A., and Brian D. Silver, "Patterns of Cohort Mortality in the Soviet Population," *Population and Development Review*, 15, 3 (September 1989), pp. 471–501.

24. United Nations, *The Determinants and Consequences of Population Trends*, p. 114.

25. United Nations, *World Population Trends and Policies*, pp. 128–129.

26. Ibid., p. 126–128.

27. Ibid., p. 126.

28. Chin, James S., S. Lwnaga, and Jonathan Mann, "The Global Epidemiology and Projected Short-Term Demographic Impact of AIDS," in *Population Bulletin of the United Nations*, no. 27, Department of International Economic and Social Affairs (New York: United Nations, 1989) 54-68.

29. Caldwell, John C., "Cultural and Social Factors Influencing Mortality Levels in Developing Countries," *The Annals of the American Academy of Political and Social Science*, 510 (July 1990), 44–59.

30. Kinsella, Kevin, "Aging in the Third World," U.S. Bureau of the Census, *International Population Reports*, Series P-95, No. 79 (Washington, DC: U.S. Government Printing Office, 1988).

31. United Nations Secretariat, "Sex Differentials in Survivorship in the Developing World: Levels, Regional Patterns and Demographic Determininants," in *Population Bulletin of the United Nations*, no. 25, Department of International Economic and Social Affairs (New York: United Nations, 1988) pp. 51-64.

32. Waldron, Ingrid, "Effects of Labor Force Participation on Sex Differences in Mortality and Morbidity," in *Women, Work, and Stress*, eds. M. Frankenhaeuser, V. Lundberg, M. Chesney (New York: Plenum Press, 1990).

33. Verbrugge, Lois, "A Life-and-Death Paradox," *American Demographics*, 10, 7 (July 1988), pp. 34–37.

34. Chin, Lwanga, and Mann, "The Global Epidemiology," pp. 54– 68.

35. Caldwell, "Cultural and Social Factors," pp. 44–59.

36. Kitagawa, Evelyn, "On Mortality," *Demography*, 14, 4 (November 1977), 381–389.

37. National Center for Health Statistics, "Annual Summary of Births, Marriages, Divorces, and Deaths: United States, 1989," *Monthly Vital Statistics Report*, 38, 13 (August 30, 1990), (Hyattsville, MD: Public Health Service), p. 25; and Randall, Teri, "Infant Mortality Receiving Increasing Attention," *Journal of the American Medical Association*, 263, 19 (May 16, 1990), pp. 2604–2605.

38. National Center for Health Statistics, "Annual Summary of Births, Marriages, Divorces, and Deaths," p. 19.

39. McCord, Colin, and Harold P. Freeman, "Excess Mortality in Harlem," *New England Journal of Medicine*, 322, 3 (January 18, 1990), 173–177.

40. National Center for Health Statistics, "Annual Summary of Births, Marriages, Divorces, and Deaths," p. 19.

41. Korenman, Sanders, Noreen Goldman, and Yuanreng Hu, "Health and Mortality Differentials by Marital Status at Older Ages: Economics and Gender," paper presented at the annual meetings of the Population Association of America, Toronto, Canada (May 1990).

42. House, James S., Karl R. Landis, Debra Umberson, "Social Relationships and Health," *Science*, 241 (July 29, 1988), 540–545.

43. The 1973 World Almanac (New York: Newspaper Enterprise Association, 1973), pp. 774–777.
44. Gorer, Geoffrey, *Death, Grief, and Mourning* (Garden City, NY: Doubleday, 1965).
45. Macionis, John J., *Sociology* (Englewood Cliffs, NJ: Prentice-Hall, 1989), p. 451.
46. U.S. Bureau of the Census, *Historical Statistics of the United States: Colonial Times to 1970*, bicentennial Ed., Part 1 (Washington, DC: U.S. Government Printing Office, 1975) p. 56; and U.S. Bureau of the Census, *Statistical Abstract of the United States 1990* (Washington, DC: U.S. Government Printing Office, 1990), p. 74.
47. Atchley, Robert C., *Social Forces and Aging*, 6th ed. (Belmont, CA: Wadsworth Publishing Company, 1991), pp. 190–191.
48. Uhlenberg, Peter, "Death and the Family," *Journal of Family History*, 5 (Autumn 1980) pp. 313–320; and Cotts, Susan, Watkins, Jane A. Menken, and John Bongaarts, "Demographic Foundations of Family Change," *American Sociological Review*, 52, 3 (June 1987), pp. 346–358.

CHAPTER 5
FERTILITY

FERTILITY MEASUREMENT

Just as demographers take great pains to measure mortality with precision, they have also developed careful measures of fertility. The crude birth rate (births per 1,000 population), while convenient, does not take into account differences in age composition. For females, the period of fecundity (the biological capacity to conceive and bear children) extends from around age 12 to beyond age 50 in developed societies, with a shorter reproductive span among women in developing societies. The fecundity of women is distinctly higher in the middle years of the reproductive period, with subfecundity characterizing adolescents and women approaching menopause.[1] Male fecundity also varies with age, although not as much as female fecundity, as individual men are capable of biological fatherhood into old age.

Even the highest recorded fertility levels—those of the Hutterites, a religious sect living in central North America near the United States–Canada border, where in 1950 women gave birth to an average of 8.9 children—is far below the hypothetical maximum of 40 births (one every 9 months) over 30 years of reproduction. In a natural fertility population, where contraception is not practiced to limit the total number of births, the average interval between live births is typically 30 months. After giving birth, women experience "postpartum amenorrhea," which literally means absence of menstruation and ovulation after childbirth. The main determinant of the length of postpartum amenorrhea is breastfeeding, in terms of both frequency and duration. Breastfeeding is not a reliable contraceptive for individuals, primarily because ovulation and menses usually return before women stop breastfeeding. For a population, however, breastfeeding can extend the length of birth intervals and therefore suppress fertility. The postpartum period averages 12 months in a natural fertility population. Another 5 months on average is spent with pregnancies that abort spontaneously, including waiting time to conceive, the pregnancy itself, and a nonsusceptible period following the loss, which is shorter than postpartum amenorrhea. The remainder of the birth interval comprises another 4 months of waiting to conceive and the 9 months of pregnancy before the live birth. In sum, women in high-fertility societies are pregnant for only about one-sixth of their reproductive years (about 5 years in total). In addition to the nonsusceptible periods (7.5 years) and waiting times to conception (4.8 years), women are sterile for an average of 5 years while married and not at risk 7.5 years while unmarried (within a 30-year reproductive span).[2]

Although it is possible to compute fertility rates for both males and females, female fertility rates are analyzed more commonly, for reasons of convention and data availability. A birth always involves a woman's presence, but it is more difficult to link every birth with a particular man. Ideally, both male and female fertility rates should be computed for populations with skewed sex ratios. Moreover, the social determinants of female fertility may not be the same as those for male fertility. Despite these reservations, fertility rates here and in other sources virtually always refer to females.

One fertility measure that improves upon the crude birth rate is the *general fertility rate*, which is the number of births per 1,000 women ages 15 to 44. This measure provides considerable, but not perfect, control for differences in age composition between two populations. The most exact fertility measures are based upon *age-specific birth rates*, the ratio of the births to women of a given age to the total number of women in that age group for each age group for which reproduction is biologically possible. The *total fertility rate* is the summation of age-specific birth rates over all the reproductive ages. The formula is as follows:

$$\sum_{x=10}^{49} b_x$$

where b_x is the number of children borne per woman of age x. A total fertility rate for a given year or set of years tells the number of children a woman would have if she went through her reproductive life experiencing the age-specific fertility rates prevailing during the particular year. A variant of the total fertility rate is the *gross reproduction rate*, which involves only female births and is computed as follows:

$$\sum_{x=10}^{49} b^f_x$$

where b^f_x is the number of female births per woman of age x. The interpretation of the gross reproduction rate is the same as the total fertility rate except that it counts only female children. The *net reproduction rate* applies survival ratios to the components of the gross reproduction rate to measure the number of daughters a woman would have if she experienced a given set of fertility and mortality rates through her childbearing years.

We have thus far presented these measures for given years, or as *period* measures. Just as we can distinguish period and cohort mortality measures, we can do the same with fertility measures. For example the *period total fertility rate* for 1990 would consist of a sum of age-specific birth rates for women of each age in 1990, whereas the total fertility rate for the birth cohort of 1939-40 would consist of a summation of the birth rate for 10-year-old girls in 1950, 11-year-old girls in 1951, and so on, up to and including 49-year-old women in 1989. Period measures tend to fluctuate more than cohort measures because the timing of births affects period fertility rates. A decline in the mean age at childbearing temporarily inflates the period total fertility rates even though there is no change in the total fertility of any birth cohort. Conversely, a rise in the average age of childbearing temporarily deflates the period rates even though there is no change for any birth cohort. The decline in the age at childbearing in the United States in the 1950s produced period fertility rates that were higher than the rates that any of the birth cohorts experienced.

Even when birth registration is imperfect, as it is in many of the developing nations, and the direct measurement of fertility lacks validity, census data can provide useful fertility information. The proportion of the total population under age 15 is a good general indicator of the level of fertility in a population; equally suitable is the ratio of children under the age of 5 to women 15 to 49 years of age. Many censuses ask women the number of children they have ever borne. The number of children ever born to women 45 to 49 years of age as determined from the census bears a very close relation to the total fertility rate for the cohort born 45 to 49 years before the census.

MECHANISMS DIRECTLY AFFECTING FERTILITY

A causal analysis of fertility may involve many factors and complication relations among the factors. Kingsley Davis and Judith Blake systematically outlined the mechanisms that directly affect fertility, through which all other factors must operate.[3] They assume that the birth of a child is not possible unless (1) sexual intercourse has occurred, (2) intercourse has resulted in pregnancy, and (3) pregnancy has been completed to successful term. Building upon these these assumptions, they devised a list of 11 variables that directly affect fertility. They term these *intermediate variables*, since any other variables that may affect fertility must ultimately act through one of these. In a parallel fashion, John Bongaarts outlined the four primary proximate determinates of fertility: marriage, contraception, lactation, and induced abortion.[4]

Intermediate Variables Affecting Fertility

I.   Factors affecting exposure to intercourse
  A.   Those governing the formation and dissolution of unions in the reproductive period
      1.   Age of entry into sexual unions
      2.   Permanent celibacy; proportion of women never entering sexual unions
      3.   Amount of reproductive period spent after or between unions
          a.   When unions are broken by divorce, separation, or desertion
          b.   When unions are broken by death of husband
  B.   Those governing the exposure to intercourse within unions
      4.   Voluntary abstinence
      5.   Involuntary abstinence (as a result of impotence, illness, and unavoidable but temporary separations)
      6.   Coital frequency (excluding periods of abstinence)
II.   Factors affecting exposure to conception
      7.   Fecundity or infecundity, as affected by involuntary causes
      8.   Use or nonuse of contraception
          a.   By mechanical and chemical means
          b.   By other means
      9.   Fecundity or infecundity, as affected by voluntary causes (sterilization, medical treatment, etc.)
III.   Factors affecting gestation and successful parturition
      10.   Fetal mortality from involuntary causes
      11.   Fetal mortality from voluntary causes

By examining historical trends and current variation for each intermediate variable, we can understand more fully how each contributes to overall fertility.

1. *Age of entry into sexual unions.*   One reason that preindustrial fertility in Europe persisted at moderate rather than high levels was that both men and women married relatively late (23 to 28 years for women) because couples were supposed to have independent means of support before entering into marriage and childbearing. In contrast, women in rural China married at 17.5 years in 1930.[5] More recent data also show variation in age at marriage. The median age at marriage for women in Bangladesh was 13.3 in 1975.[6] In 1987, Japanese women married at 25.3 years, on average.[7]

Of course, a sexual union can take place outside of marriage, and in many countries, large proportions of unmarried women are sexually active. For example, in 1988, two-thirds of never-married women in the United States had experienced a sexual relationship.[8] In parts of Latin America, consensual unions take the place of legal, formal marriages for large segments of society.

2. *Permanent celibacy.*   Not only did men and women marry relatively late in preindustrial Western Europe, but large proportions (10 percent or more) were still single at age 50. The combination of late marriage and high proportions never

marrying reduced potential fertility by more than half. In other preindustrial societies, such as those in Asia and Africa, marriage has been nearly universal (and early), so that only 10 to 15 percent of potential fertility is lost due to women ages 15 to 50 not being married.

3. *Amount of reproductive period spent after or between unions.*   In most preindustrial populations, fertility outside of marriage is relatively small, with the major exceptions of Caribbean and Latin American societies, where consensual unions may be more common than legal marriage. In Jamaica in the 1950s, consensual unions broke up frequently, for reasons of incompatibility or because the woman did not want to risk the chance of another pregnancy.[9] Western populations have generally experienced either little marital disruption (historically) or in recent times, higher levels of marital disruption in conjunction with relatively high rates of remarriage, particularly for younger women, so that Western societies experience only a small proportion of fertility loss due to time spent between sexual unions. In the early 1900s, women in India experienced a fertility loss of about 12 percent because of high rates of widowhood and the taboo on remarriage for widows.[10]

4. *Voluntary abstinence.*   Almost all societies observe a period of abstinence during late pregnancy and during the postpartum period. Some sub-Saharan African societies practice extended abstinence of more than 1 year in order to space births, which they recognize as increasing the chance of child survival.[11] Periodic abstinence is a method of birth control that relies on couples refraining from intercourse around the time of ovulation, using basal temperature, cervical mucus, or calendar calculations to determine ovulation, with the first two methods producing greater accuracy.

5. *Involuntary abstinence.*   In some societies, notably Bangladesh and Peru, large proportions of men migrate seasonally for agricultural work, and as a result, women's conception rates fluctuate from one month to another. In the absence of the seasonal migration, fertility could increase by as much as 25 percent.[12]

6. *Frequency of intercourse.*   Much theoretical evidence suggests that this variable may be rather important in determining differences in fertility between individuals. Whether or not it affects the fertility of various populations is another matter. It is possible, however, that factors such as diet, temperature, humidity, and the prevalence of certain enervating diseases may affect the average frequency of sexual intercourse in different populations. In the United States, coital frequency declines with age and duration of marriage.[13]

7. *Fecundity or infecundity as affected by involuntary causes.*   Several factors may affect the likelihood of conception, given that intercourse occurs on a regular basis. One of the most significant factors that can have both temporary and permanent effects on fecundity is disease. Historically, tuberculosis and smallpox produced subfecundity in Europe before 1900 and among U.S. African-Americans in the nineteenth and early twentieth centuries. In Central African societies, widespread, untreated diseases have resulted in relatively low fertility levels and high rates of childlessness in the absence of contraception.[14] Sexually transmitted

diseases, such as syphillis, gonorrhea, chlamydia, and other diseases that directly attack the reproductive system can cause permanent sterility in both men and women if untreated.

Poor nutrition can also produce subfecundity by inhibiting ovulation. The onset of menstruation is in part indirectly related to levels of body fat, one possible reason for relatively low ages of menarche among well-fed girls in developed societies. Because of the demands that breastfeeding places on a woman's body, lactational infecundity may last longer in poorly fed women.[15]

Subfecundity in developed societies has received more attention with the increasing trend of later marriage and childbearing. The probability of conceiving declines gradually until age 35, and then more rapidly in the late 30s and early 40s. The changing age patterns of marriage and childbearing have resulted in proportionately more women being unable to conceive at the right time for them. While contraception allows women to control their maximum level of fertility, there is no comparably effective treatment for overcoming subfecundity.[16]

8. *Use or nonuse of contraception.* No other intermediate variable or proximate determinant has affected the decline of fertility more than contraception. Even before the demographic transition, humans practiced contraception, although not on the same scale as today.[17] Contraception refers to any behavior that is used to deliberately keep a woman from conceiving, so that the intention is theoretically as important as the outcome. For example, breastfeeding is not considered contraceptive behavior unless its primary purpose is to inhibit ovulation. The Davis-Blake framework considers periodic abstinence and contraceptive sterilization in other categories, although many fertility studies consider them to be forms of contraception.

One of the simplest contraceptive techniques, coitus interruptus (that is, withdrawal of the penis from the vagina just before ejaulation), is mentioned in the Old Testament. Along with abstinence, it accounted for most of the fertility decline in Western Europe.[18] A condom made of linen was invented in the sixteenth century, although even the early Egyptians used "penis protectors" to prevent disease. Latex condoms appeared in the 1930s, less expensive and more effective than their rubber predecessors. For hundreds of years, women in many societies attempted to block sperm from entering the cervical opening by inserting sponges or even leaves. The infamous Casanova gave his lovers empty lemon halves to use as diaphragms. Not until the 1880s, when the modern diaphragm was invented, did this method become highly effective. In 1988, approximately 13 percent of U.S. women ages 15 to 44 were using the condom or diaphragm.[19]

The modern contraceptive revolution took hold in the 1960s, with the widespread acceptance of two new methods—the oral contraceptive (the pill) and the intrauterine device (IUD). For the first time, reversible contraception was coitus-independent and approached 100 percent effectiveness when used properly. By 1988, some 30 percent of U.S. women ages 15 to 24 were using the pill, up from 24 percent in 1982. Among women 25 to 34 years of age, slightly more than one-fifth used the pill in 1988, an increase from the 1982 level of 17 percent. Relatively few women ages 35 to 44 were using the pill in 1988. Most women in this age group have completed childbearing, making sterilization an attractive option for them. Approximately 16 percent of women 35 to 44 used reversible contraceptive methods other than the pill and IUD. The IUD never achieved levels of use as high as those for the pill in the United States, although family-planning programs in some Asian countries distributed it more than any other method, probably because once inserted, the wearer does not need to make any further contraceptive efforts, apart from occasionally checking the location.[20]

Since the development of the pill, variations of it have been developed and used on a fairly large scale. Instead of taking a pill on a daily basis, women in some parts of the world have access to an injectable contraceptive, given monthly. The most recent innovation is a contraceptive drug implanted under the skin in thin metal rods that can provide protection for up to 5 years.

Not only in the United States and other developed nations is contraception a universal phenomenon; it has permeated societies in much of the developed world as well. Virtually all women in East Asia and Latin America had heard about contraception by the mid 1980s. Only in certain South Asian and African nations did fewer than one-half of all women know of at least one contraceptive method. More than two-thirds of all married women in most Latin American and East Asian nations had used contraception (including sterilization) at some time in their lives.[21]

9. *Fecundity or infecundity as affected by voluntary causes.* The most important factor causing (temporary) infecundity is lactation, with both the intensity and the duration of breastfeeding affecting ovulation. While some Western populations have very short periods of breastfeeding that include supplemental foods (hence reducing the intensity) and many women not choosing to breastfeed, long periods of lactation with little or no supplemental foods characterize other populations, where lactational infecundity can last more than 18 months.[22]

Sterilization, often considered contraception, provides a permanent solution to family planning, and can be carried out on either men or women. Female sterilization, tubal ligation, is a more costly and complicated surgical procedure than vasectomy, or male sterilization. In 1988, female sterilization was still more widespread than male sterilization in the United States, particularly among African-Americans. Thirty percent of all women ages 15 to 44 (or their partners) had been sterilized, and among women ages 35 to 44, close to 60 percent chose sterilization.[23] Around 1980, almost one-third of all "contraceptive use" in the world involved sterilization, and it was more widespread in developing countries, most notably China and India.

10. *Fetal mortality from involuntary causes.* On average, between 20 and 25 percent of all known pregnancies are spontaneously aborted, although an estimated 60 percent of fertilized ova do not continue to live births. More than half of these abort before a menstrual period is delayed. Even though researchers agree that there is wide variation among individuals, most assume that spontaneous abortion rates do not vary from one population to another. Higher-order pregnancies

and pregnancies among older women carry a greater risk of fetal loss. Women who experience a spontaneous abortion are more likely than other women to have further losses.[24]

11. *Fetal mortality from voluntary causes.*   Induced abortion is one of the most significant means of birth control, even though it is not considered contraception. While abortions have been practiced throughout human history with varying levels of safety, modern methods make induced abortion a safe procedure for women when performed under sanitary conditions. When abortion is illegal, it is often carried out under poor conditions and can result in serious health problems and even death.

Among developing countries, East Asian women had the most widespread access to induced abortion in 1982, with African women having the lowest levels of access.[25] In the United States in 1987, among 14 states reporting this information, there were 338 abortions per 1,000 live births, a slight decrease from both 1985 and 1986.[26]

FERTILITY TRENDS

Before the demographic transition, fertility levels in northern and western Europe were only moderately high (crude birth rates less than 40 per 1,000 and total fertility rates of about 5 children per woman), primarily because of relatively late marriage and relatively high proportions of never-married persons, although even marital fertility was lower than the Hutterite level, suggesting some form of birth control or more extensive breastfeeding than the Hutterites practiced.[27] The incipient decline took place in France during the 1830s, followed by most of the other northern and western European countries in the latter part of the nineteenth century. Birth rates were higher in the United States and Canada before the fertility decline, which began there in the early twentieth century. The trend of declining fertility spread to Southern and Eastern Europe during the 1920s and 1930s, continuing to the Soviet Union in the 1940s and Japan by the 1950s. Argentina, Uruguay, and Israel also experienced fertility declines before their neighboring countries did.[28] Figure 5–1 shows the long-term fertility decline among the white population in the United States, from 1800 to 1990, which was interrupted by the 1946–1964 "baby boom."[29] This figure demonstrates that the baby boom was an anomaly and that the low fertility that followed it has been part of a long-term trend.

In the 1960s, crude birth rates fell below 30 per 1,000 in Taiwan, Hong Kong, Mauritius, Puerto Rico, Singapore, and Trinidad and Tobago.[30] Until the late 1970s, fertility levels and trends in other developing countries were not well documented, and so the World Fertility Survey was established in 1972 to design and implement fertility surveys all over the world. Between 1973 and 1982, 62 countries representing almost 40 percent of the world's population had participated in this global undertaking. The surveys showed that by 1980, fertility had declined significantly in large areas of Asia, Latin America, and the Middle East, although most of those countries still had fertility levels twice those of the more developed countries.

Total Fertility Rates, 1800-1990
U.S. White Population

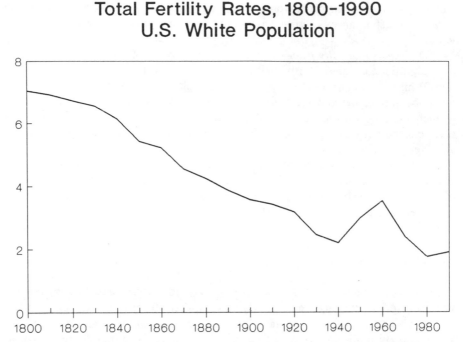

Figure 5-1. Total fertility rate for the white population of the United States, 1800–1990. *Sources*: Rates
from 1800 to 1960 are in adapted form from Coale, Ansley J., and Melvin Zelnik, *New
Estimates of Fertility and Population in the United States* (Princeton, NJ: Princeton
University Press, 1963), copyright © 1963 by Princeton University Press, selections from
Table 2, p. 36 used with permission; rates for 1970 and 1980 are from National Center for
Health Statistics, "Advance Report of Final Natality Statistics, 1988," *Monthly Vital
Statistics Report*, vol. 39, no. 4, suppl. (Hyattsville: MD: Public Health Service, 1990); the
rate for 1990 is estimated from Haub, Carl, et al., *1990 World Population Data Sheet*
(Washington, DC: Population Reference Bureau, 1990).

Sub-Saharan African nations had not experienced any decline in fertility, with
reproduction at over 8 children per woman in many countries.[31]

Throughout the 1980s, sub-Saharan African fertility rates remained high,
although moderate declines took place in northern Africa. Latin American total
fertility rates fell by almost one-fifth overall in the 1980s, with the largest declines
in Central America, where fertility was the highest in the region. Even though
fertility declined overall, Latin American countries showed wide variation in
fertility by the end of the 1980s. One of the subregions in Latin America with the
greatest fertility declines is the Caribbean, although in 1982-83, Haiti had a total
fertility rate of 6.2 children per woman. Some Latin American countries experienced increases in the crude birth rate during the 1980s, probably because of
increasing numbers of persons in the reproductive ages.[32]

As with Latin America, fertility trends vary widely among Asian societies. In
Singapore and Hong Kong, fertility continued to decline and went below 2 children
per woman during the 1980s. Between the mid 1960s and mid 1980s, fertility fell

rapidly in many East Asian countries, including Thailand and South Korea, and also in one notable South Asian country, Sri Lanka. The most phenomenal fertility decline in human history must be that of the People's Republic of China, where in the late 1960s women were having more than six children on average. By 1980 the total fertility rate reached 2.2, although changes in the marriage laws led to a slight increase in fertility during the early 1980s.[33]

Declining fertility usually refers to a decrease in the crude birth rate or number of children per woman, both of which are measures of quantity. In addition, fertility declines also involve changes in the timing of childbearing. The pace of childbearing varied among pretransition societies because of differences in the timing of marriage and the duration and intensity of breastfeeding. With the transition to lower levels of fertility, contraception also affected the timing of childbearing.[34] The fertility transition in German villages consisted primarily of women ending their childbearing years earlier, as shown by the declining age at last birth between 1750 and 1900.[35] In nineteenth-century Utah, the fertility decline consisted of both stopping childbearing earlier and spacing births further apart.[36] The rapid fertility decline in Korea during the 1960s and 1970s resulted in fewer children per woman but a faster pace of childbearing in the early part of marriage. Premarital conceptions rose, thus shortening the interval between marriage and the first birth. The interval between the first and second births also became shorter due to a decline in breastfeeding and possibly a desire for couples to concentrate childbearing and childrearing into a shorter time period.[37] The baby bust in the United States during the 1970s involved delayed marriage and even further delays in first births after marriage. The proportion of women ages 25 to 34 with no children increased by 56 percent between 1970 and 1982.[38]

FACTORS AFFECTING THE DECISION TO HAVE CHILDREN

The 11 intermediate variables outlined by Davis and Blake explain the biological mechanisms leading to a live birth—exposure to intercourse, likelihood of conception, and the likelihood of a pregnancy resulting in a live birth. They do not, however, address the decision-making process that we in a modern society take for granted. Until reliable contraceptives were developed, many people considered fertility to be out of their control, just as mortality was. Explanations for declining fertility tend to focus on changes in marital fertility—the factors leading married couples to produce smaller families.

Ansley Coale lists three prerequisites for a sizable decline in marital fertility.[39] First, fertility control must be considered *acceptable*, rather than immoral. Second, lower fertility must provide *advantages*, both social and economic, to individual families. Third, methods of fertility reduction must be *available*. The first prerequisite addresses normative issues—that is, the question of whether a society sees fertility control as immoral or even illegal. The second prerequisite is concerned with economic issues. Couples will not decide to have fewer children unless they perceive it to be in their better interest to do so. The third prerequisite is a matter of technology and distribution. Methods of effective birth control must exist, and couples must be able to obtain them.

Richard Easterlin addresses the economic aspects of fertility decision-making with an economic model consisting of three variables: demand for children, potential supply of children (if fertility were not controlled), and the costs of fertility regulation.[40] The demand for children involves balancing household income with the costs of raising children, within the context of subjective "tastes." While economists tend to focus more on the first two variables, price and income, sociologists have analyzed "tastes," which translate into the norms regarding family size and child-rearing expectations. The costs of fertility control include the direct financial costs, the inconvenience of obtaining the method and using it, and any emotional costs of using contraception.

Another economic perspective on the fertility decline was posed by Caldwell, who analyzed how the value of children changed with modernization.[41] He noted that in premodern societies, wealth tends to flow up from the younger generation to the older generation. Children are valuable to their parents when they are young because they can provide agricultural labor. When their parents are old, children provide economic security and ensure that the family lineage will endure. With modernization, the direction of wealth flow tends to reverse. Children in a modern society do not tend to contribute to the family's economic well-being; rather, they are net consumers, especially because of the need for many years of education in a modern society. Because modern societies tend to provide some means of old-age economic security, children are not necessary for this purpose. As intergenerational wealth shifts from an upward flow to a downward flow, large numbers of children become less desirable, and fertility decreases. Because sub-Saharan African social structure has continued to place a high level of significance on preserving family lineages and allocates the cost of children among many adults, individual women have not yet found it to their advantage to limit the number of children they bear. In all other parts of the developing world, fertility control has started to become acceptable.[42]

Small families are not only more beneficial to parents in a modern society, but they also contribute to higher levels of achievement for children. Using data from multiple social surveys, Judith Blake convincingly demonstrates that children from small families have higher levels of achievement, particularly as measured by years of education completed, even after controlling for the effects of other social and economic variables.[43] Data from the developing countries are less conclusive. At the beginning of the development process, family size and education may be positively associated; however, as fertility declines and a society becomes more modern, family size becomes negatively associated with children's educational achievement. Another indicator of child quality is health, and child mortality appears to be lower in small families.[44]

Improvements in socioeconomic development are incontrovertibly associated with declines in fertility, both historically and currently. At the macro-level, societies that have greater levels of urbanization, industrialization, and literacy, as well as lower infant and child mortality, tend to experience earlier fertility declines. Similar findings hold at the individual level as well. Better educated urban women who work in the paid labor force tend to have lower fertility rates. Socioeconomic development, however, cannot explain the speed with which a fertility decline spreads throughout a society. Furthermore, fertility transitions have tended to progress more rapidly in culturally homogeneous countries (such as England and Thailand) than in nations with more ethnic diversity (such as Switzerland and India). A common language in particular appears to hasten a fertility decline once it has taken hold. These findings suggest that in addition to socioeconomic development, social networks are integral to a fertility decline. Like other social movements, a fertility decline diffuses through a population both by word of mouth and by means of central media sources—for example, newspapers, radio, and television. It is difficult to test the salience of a social network hypothesis of fertility decline because many of the available indicators of social ties are also related to socioeconomic development. Individuals with a high degree of integration into society also tend to have high levels of socioeconomic status. They read newspapers, work in the industrial labor force, and live in cities. Whereas a socioeconomic explanation of these persons' adoption of low fertility behavior emphasizes the costs and benefits of reproductive decisions, a social network explanation argues that well-integrated persons are more likely to embrace societal norms and values.[45]

FACTORS AFFECTING UNINTENDED PREGNANCY AND CHILDBEARING

Explanations for declines in marital fertility tend to emphasize the ways in which fertility preferences change. Even in the most modern settings, however, fertility outcomes are not a perfect reflection of preferences, because contraception is not perfect. Even if used accurately, all contraceptives (except total abstinence and sterilization) fail on occasion. Therefore, most studies of contraceptive effectiveness analyze "use effectiveness," which include failures in using the method, as well as failures inherent in the method under ideal use. One reason that barrier methods, like the condom and diaphragm, are less effective than the pill is that barrier methods require use at the time of intercourse, which couples may not always do. Condom failures, for example, include pregnancies due to defective condoms as well as to inaccurate use and non-use.

Unintended pregnancies comprise failures in either timing or number. Early family-planning programs typically targeted their services to women who wanted no more children or who had reached a certain parity.[46] Not surprisingly, studies in numerous settings show that use effectiveness increases as couples attain their desired family size.[47] Survey data from 48 developing countries during the 1970s and 1980s suggest that, on average, one-fourth of all births were unwanted. Countries in the early and late stages of the demographic transition had the lowest levels of unwanted fertility, and countries in the middle of their transition had the highest levels of unwanted fertility.[48]

While contraception may be widely available in most developed countries, substantial proportions of women in developing countries may want to use contraception but may be unable to obtain it. The "unmet need for family planning services" varies from country to country and within particular countries as well. A study of contraceptive use in five Latin American countries revealed levels of unmet need ranging from 15 percent in Brazil and Colombia to 21 percent in the Dominican Republic, 25 percent in Ecuador, and 29 percent in Peru. Unmet need for contraception is greater among women who want to cease childbearing rather than delay their next birth. Rural women, younger women, and women with lower levels of education tend to have the greatest levels of unmet need for contraception.[49]

Unintended pregnancies are of particular concern among adolescents, although in some developing countries, women are expected to consummate sexual unions shortly after reaching puberty and to begin childbearing as soon as possible. In more developed countries, most teenagers are discouraged from having children, as societies tend to view early motherhood as incompatible with finishing one's education and getting started on the road to a successful future. Even in developing countries, teenage childbearing may not be condoned in urban areas, for these same reasons. Teenage pregnancies are more likely than pregnancies to women in their 20s to result in health problems for the young mother and her child. Teenagers who give birth often leave school before graduating, which results in their having fewer employment options. While most developed countries provide some (although often not enough) assistance for adolescent mothers and their children, few developing countries can support teenage mothers and their children.[50]

Among developed countries, teenage pregnancy and childbearing is the most widespread in the United States. While adolescent fertility has declined in the United States (as in other developed countries), it is still much higher than in most European countries and other developed nations. In 1980 there were 96 pregnancies for every 1,000 teenagers in the United States, and 83 for every 1,000 white U.S. teens. In contrast, the pregnancy rate was 43 in France, 44 in Canada, 35 in Sweden, and 14 in the Netherlands. Even though the fertility rates of African-American teenagers are higher than those of whites, this does not explain the vast difference between the United States and other countries. The other countries tend to have more available contraceptive services for teenagers, whereas in the United States, there is widespread belief that giving teenagers greater access to birth control will increase their rate of sexual activity. Generous welfare benefits are another factor thought to encourage teenage childbearing; yet the other countries have more extensive social welfare programs than those in the United States. The conclusion reached by a group of researchers studying adolescent pregnancy in these developed countries was that U.S. teens receive conflicting messages about sex. Various media portray sex as glamorous and exciting, yet teens receive little or no information about contraception or the problems of early parenthood; rather, they are supposed to just say no to sex. As a result, the United States must deal with relatively high rates of adolescent pregnancy, childbirth, and abortion.[51]

NOTES

1. McFalls, Joseph, "Frustrated Fertility: A Population Paradox, *Population Bulletin*, 34, 2, (Washington, DC: Population Reference Bureau, Inc., 1979), pp. 3–10.
2. Bongaarts, John, "Why High Birth Rates Are So Low," *Population and Development Review*, 1, 2 (December 1975), 289–296.
3. Davis, Kingsley, and Judith Blake, "Social Structure and Fertility: An Analytic Framework," *Economic Development and Cultural Change*, 4, 4 (1956), 211–235.
4. Bongaarts, John, "A Framework for Analyzing the Proximate Determinants of Fertility," *Population and Development Review*, 4, 1 (March 1978), 105–132.
5. Coale, Ansley J., "The Decline of Fertility in Europe since the Eighteenth Century as a Chapter in Demographic History," in *The Decline of Fertility in Europe*, eds. Ansley J. Coale and Susan Cotts Watkins (Princeton, NJ: Princeton University Press, 1986), pp. 1–30.
6. Lightbourne, Robert, Jr., and Susheela Singh, with Cynthia P. Green, "The World Fertility Survey: Charting Global Childbearing," *Population Bulletin*, 37, 1, (Washington, DC: Population Reference Bureau, March 1982).
7. United Nations, *1988 Demographic Yearbook* (New York: United Nations, 1990), p. 561.
8. Forrest, Jaqueline Darroch, and Susheela Singh, "The Sexual and Reproductive Behavior of American Women, 1982–1988," *Family Planning Perspectives*, 22, 5 (September–October 1990), 206–214.
9. Blake, Judith, *Family Structure in Jamaica: The Social Context of Reproduction* (New York: Free Press, 1961).
10. Coale, "The Decline of Fertility in Europe."
11. Lesthaeghe, R., H. J. Page, and O. Adegbola, "Child-Spacing and Fertility in Lagos," in *Child-Spacing in Tropical Africa: Traditions and Change*, eds. Hilary J. Page and Ron Lesthaeghe (London: Academic Press, 1981), pp. 147–179.
12. Menken, Jane, "Seasonal Migration and Seasonal Variation in Fecundability: Effects on Birth Rates and Birth Intervals," *Demography*, 16, 1 (February 1979), 103–119; and Heer, David M., "Fertility Differences Between Indian and Spanish-Speaking Parts of Andean Countries," *Population Studies*, 18, 1 (July 1964), 71–84.
13. Trussell, J., and C. F. Westoff, "Contraceptive Practice and Trends in Coital Frequency," *Family Planning Perspectives*, 12, 5 (September–October 1980), 246–249.
14. McFalls, "Frustrated Fertility," pp. 3–10.
15. Coale, Ansley, "The History of Human Population," in *The Human Population*, "A Scientific American Book" (San Francisco: W. H. Freeman & Company, 1974), pp. 15–25.
16. Menken, Jane, "Age and Fertility: How Late Can You Wait," *Demography*, 22, 4 (November 1985), 469–483.
17. For a complete account of the early history of contraceptive practices, see Himes, Norman, *Medical History of Contraception* (New York: Gamut Press, 1963 [orig. 1936]). Westoff, Leslie Aldridge, and Charles F. Westoff, *From Now to Zero: Fertility, Contraception, and Abortion in America* (Boston: Little, Brown, & Company, 1968), provide a further review of contraception. These two sources provide most of the information contained in this section.
18. Knodel, John, and Etinenne van de Walle, "Lessons from the Past: Policy Implications of Historical Fertility Studies," in *The Decline of Fertility in Europe*, eds. Coale and Watkins, pp. 390–419.
19. Mosher, William D., and William F. Pratt, "Contraceptive Use in the United States, 1973–88," *Advance Data from Vital and Health Statistics*, no. 182 (Hyattsville, MD: National Center for Health Statistics, 1990).

20. Ibid.
21. United Nations, Department of International Economic and Social Affairs, *World Population: Trends and Policies, 1987 Monitoring Report*, Population Studies no. 103 (New York: United Nations, 1988), pp. 71–81.
22. Bongaarts, "A Framework," pp. 105–132.
23. Mosher and Pratt, "Contraceptive Use."
24. Casterline, John, "Maternal Age, Gravidity, and Pregnancy Spacing Effects on Spontaneous Fetal Mortality." *Social Biology*, 36, 3–4 (1989), 186–212.
25. United Nations, *World Population: Trends and Policies*, p. 95.
26. Kochanek, Kenneth D., "Induced Terminations of Pregnancy: Reporting States, 1987." *Monthly Vital Statistics Report*, 38, 9, suppl. (Hyattsville, MD: Public Health Service, National Center for Health Statistics, 1990).
27. Coale, "The Decline of Fertility," pp. 1–30.
28. United Nations, Department of Economic and Social Affairs, *The Determinants and Consequences of Population Trends: New Summary of Findings on Interaction of Demographic, Economic and Social Factors*, vol. 1, Population Studies no. 50 (New York: United Nations, 1973), p. 65.
29. Figure 5–1 presents fertility rates for only the white population because the data for other ethnic groups, notably African-Americans, have not been of sufficient quality until recent decades.
30. United Nations, *The Determinants and Consequences of Population Trends*, p. 65.
31. Lightbourne, et al., "The World Fertility Survey: Charting Global Childbearing."
32. United Nations, *World Population: Trends and Policies*, pp. 50–51.
33. Ibid., p. 52.
34. Watkins, Susan, "The Fertility Transition: Europe and the Third World Compared," *Sociological Forum*, 2, 4 (Autumn 1987), 645–673.
35. Knodel, John, "Starting, Stopping, and Spacing During the Early Stages of Fertility Transition: The Experience of German Village Populations in the Eighteenth and Nineteenth Centuries," *Demography*, 24, 2 (May 1987), 143–162.
36. Anderton, Douglas L., and Lee L. Bean, "Birth Spacing and Fertility Limitation: A Behavioral Analysis of Nineteenth Century Population," *Demography*, 22, 2 (May 1985), 169–183.
37. Rindfuss, R. R., L. L. Bumpass, J. A. Palmore, and Dae Woo Han, "The Transformation of Korean Child-Spacing Practices," *Population Studies*, 36, 1 (March 1982), 87–103.
38. Baldwin, Wendy H., and Christine Winquist Nord, "Delayed Childbearing in the U.S.: Facts and Fictions," *Population Bulletin*, 39, 4, (Washington, DC: Population Reference Bureau, November 1984).
39. Coale, Ansley J., "The Demographic Transition," in *Population Debate* (New York: United Nations, 1975), pp. 347–355.
40. Easterlin, Richard, "An Economic Framework for Fertility Analysis," *Studies in Family Planning*, 6, 3 (March 1975), 54–63.
41. Caldwell, John C., "Toward a Restatement of Demographic Transition Theory," *Population and Development Review*, 2, 3–4 (December 1976), 321–366.
42. Caldwell, John C., and Pat Caldwell, "High Fertility in Sub-Saharan Africa," *Scientific American*, 262, 5 (May 1990), 118–125.
43. Blake, Judith, *Family Size and Achievement* (Berkeley: University of California Press, 1989).
44. Knodel, John, Napaporn Havanon, Werasit Sittitrai, "Family Size and the Education of Children in the Context of Rapid Fertility Decline," *Population and Development Review*, 16, 1 (March 1990), 31–62; National Academy of Sciences, *Population Growth and Economic Development: Policy Questions* (Washington, DC: National Academy Press, 1986), p. 55.
45. Watkins, "The Fertility Transition," pp. 645–673.

46. Brackett, J. W., "Family Planning in Four Latin American Countries. Knowledge, Use, and Unmet Need: Some Findings From the WFS," *International Family Planning Perspectives and Digest*, 4, 4 (Winter 1978), 116–123.

47. Westoff, Charles F., et al., *Family Growth in Metropolitan America* (Princeton, NJ: Princeton University Press, 1961); Freedman, Ronald, and John Y. Takeshita, *Family Planning in Taiwan: An Experiment in Social Change* (Princeton, NJ: Princeton University Press, 1969); Palmore, James A., and M. B. Concepcion, "Desired Family Size and Contraceptive Use: An Eleven-Country Comparison," *International Family Planning Perspectives*, 7, 1 (March 1981), 37–40.

48. Bongaarts, John, "The Measurement of Wanted Fertility," *Population and Development Review*, 16, 3 (September 1990), 487–506.

49. Westoff, Charles F., "The Potential Demand for Family Planning: A New Measure of Unmet Need and Estimates for Five Latin American Countries," *International Family Planning Perspectives*, 14, 2 (June 1988), 45–53.

50. Crews, Kimberly A., "Teenage Parents: A Global Perspective," (Washington, DC: Population Reference Bureau, June 1989).

51. Jones, Elise F., et al., "Teenage Pregnancy in Developed Countries: Determinants and Policy Implications," *Family Planning Perspectives*, 17, 2 (March–April 1985), 53–63.

CHAPTER 6
MIGRATION

MIGRATION MEASUREMENT

Measuring migration is somewhat more complicated than gauging fertility or mortality. To measure shifts in usual place of residence from an origin to a destination, several considerations must be taken into account. First, the "usual place of residence" must be defined. Although this is no problem for most individuals, an explicit definition is necessary to cover persons with more than one "usual residence," such as college students, members of the armed forces, inmates of institutions, and seasonal migrants (such as migrant workers or retired persons who move temporarily to warmer climates in the winter).

Second, careful definitions of the "place of origin" and "place of destination" are necessary. Because a change of residence can involve anything from moving next door to moving across an ocean, the number of migrants will depend on the definition of a move. In the United States, for example, the number of persons who change households is much greater every year than the number who move to a new county; and that number, in turn, is larger than the number who move to a different state. The U.S. Bureau of the Census distinguishes between migrants and movers; *migrants* are persons who move to a new county; *movers* are those who move to a new household within a county. Another common distinction is made between *international migrants*, persons who move between nations, and *internal migrants*, those who move within a nation. Persons who enter a country are called *immigrants*, while persons who leave a country are *emigrants*. Within national boundaries, persons entering a state or region are *in-migrants*, and persons leaving a state or region are *out-migrants*.

A third consideration is whether to measure the total number of moves during a given time period or merely the change in place of residence, if any, from the beginning to the end of the period. Most migration analysts are content with the latter measurement, even though with its use, the number of residence changes in a relatively long period, such as 5 years, will be smaller than the sum of the number of changes of residence recorded each year during that period.

In addition to measuring the total number of persons who have moved to a different place, migration specialists also examine where the migrants were going and whence they had come. For the 50 states and the District of Columbia (making 51 units), there are a total of 2,550 possible *migration streams*, each characterized by a different state of origin and destination. For any given state there are 50 different streams of out-migrants and 50 streams of in-migrants. The *gross migration* between place A and place B is the sum of the number of in-migrants to A from B and the number of out-migrants from A to B. The *net migration* for place A from place B is the difference between the number of in-migrants to A from B and the number of out-migrants from A to B.

While there is only one crude birth rate and one crude death rate, there are several *crude rates of migration*, the number of migrants during the year divided by the midyear population of the total area. The *crude out-migration rate* is the number of out-migrants from a place divided by that place's midyear population. Similarly, the *crude rate of in-migration* is the number of in-migrants to a place divided by the midyear population of that place. The *net migration rate* is perhaps the most commonly computed migration rate. It is simply the ratio of the net migration to the midyear population. As with birth and death rates, migration rates may be standardized for age and sex, although the requisite migration data are more difficult to obtain.

Migration data can come from censuses, surveys, or registration, the latter being the most complete. Because most nations register the movement of individuals across borders, international migration data come from registration systems. Several nations, including Sweden, have a compulsory registration of all internal movements as well. To measure internal migration in the United States, however, we must resort to census and survey data, which ask persons where they lived at some earlier date. Migration data gathered in this way slightly underestimate the total amount of movement because they ignore persons who move and then die before the time of survey. For nations with low mortality rates, this bias is small except for the oldest age groups. More important, census and survey data usually count only one move per individual. Furthermore, an individual who is living in the same place as he or she did at some earlier date may have moved away in the intervening time and then returned, a change that census or survey would not detect.

INTERNATIONAL MIGRATION STREAMS

Humans beings have migrated since the beginnings of their existence. One of the earliest streams of migration with historical significance for European societies was the westward movement of nomadic societies in Europe and Central Asia coincident with the fall of the Roman Empire. The many societies that moved westward during this period included those speaking Celtic, Germanic, and Ural-Altaic languages. As the easternmost groups moved westward, they pushed forward those in front of them. One possible explanation for this extensive migration is that the grasslands of Central Asia dried up. A second theory is that an expanding Chinese empire disrupted the life of the nomadic groups near its borders and thus provoked the movement of all the other societies.[1]

The European and African migration to North America, South America, and Oceania began slowly after Columbus's voyage to America. An estimated 60 million Europeans left for overseas destinations. *Net migration*, however, was lower, since many of those leaving Europe later returned.[2] The migration from Africa to the New World was almost wholly a forced migration of slaves. The first slaves were brought to the colony of Virginia in 1619, and in the United States the slave trade was not abolished until 1808. During the period of slave trade, about 400,000 Africans were brought to the United States, and in 1790, 20 percent of the 4 million persons in the United States were of African descent.[3]

As industrialization spread through Europe between 1800 and 1925, considerable numbers of people were pushed off the land and emigrated to Argentina, Australia, Canada, New Zealand, or the United States, sparsely settled areas with high labor demands.[4] Statistics on immigration into the United States from abroad are available beginning in 1820. The absolute number of persons moving into the nation reached a peak in 1907, when about 1,300,000 immigrants entered the country. However, there have been several major peaks in the rate of immigration into the United States. In 1854, when 428,000 immigrants entered the United States, the rate of immigration was 16.1 per thousand U.S. population. In contrast, the immigration rate in 1907, the year with the largest numbers of immigrants, was 14.8 per thousand. The early peak period was primarily the "old migration," predominantly comprising the Irish, leaving their native land because of the potato famine, and Germans, often leaving as political refugees. The second peak period, around the turn of the twentieth century, comprised the "new migration," immigrants from Italy and Eastern Europe.[5]

In the first decade of the twentieth century, the rate of immigration from Europe into the United States was 9.2 per thousand U.S. population, and the emigration rate from Europe to the United States was about 2 per thousand.[6] Thus, in general, the trans-Atlantic migration had considerably more effect on the population of the United States than on that of Europe. However, the emigration rate from Europe to the United States varied considerably from nation to nation and from time to time. During the decade of the Irish potato famine (from 1845 to 1854), the emigration from Ireland to the United States was extremely heavy; about 1.4 million Irish emigrated to the United States from a population that had been in 1841 only a little more than 8 million.[7]

World War I brought to an end the massive migrations from European nations. The United States and other receiving countries passed laws restricting immigration, and the Great Depression of the 1930s stifled international migration, except for some return migration to Europe. Until the end of World War II, migrants tended to be predominantly political or religious refugees, rather than those seeking economic improvements.[8]

Human migrations began to reach a larger scale in the period shortly before World War II, when Jewish refugees escaped Germany, Poland, and other European countries. The related migration into Israel following World War II is noteworthy because it illustrates an extremely high rate of immigration. In 1948, the population of Israel was 650,000. By 1961, after the influx of more than 1 million immigrants, it had risen to 2.2 million.[9]

Perhaps the world's largest gross interchange in a short time span took place in India and Pakistan following the 1947 partition of British India and the establishment of these two areas as independent states. In the face of violent coercion, Hindus and Sikhs in Pakistan were forced to move to India, and Moslems in India to Pakistan. From 1947 through 1950, 10 million persons migrated from Pakistan to India, and 7.5 million from India to Pakistan.[10]

Beginning in the 1950s, international migration became global, as more nations became senders and receivers of migrants. The most significant change, however, was that Europe shifted from being a net sender to becoming an important receiver of migrants from Third World countries. The major areas of emigration included Africa, Asia, and Latin America, and included political refugees and migrants motivated by economic concerns.[11] Over 1 million refugees fled Indochina between 1975 and 1981. Almost half emigrated to the United States; large numbers also went to China, Canada, France, and Australia. Over 100,000 Kampucheans remained in refugee camps in Thailand, waiting for a receiving country to take them.[12]

In the twentieth century, the most significant international migration stream to the United States has come from Mexico. Initially, around 1900, migrants left Mexico because of changing economic conditions there: Common agricultural lands were enclosed and the large landowners began to replace labor with capital, leaving many landless Mexicans without a means of subsistence. At the same time, the southwestern United States experienced economic growth with the arrival of railroads, linking that region to the rest of the country and to Mexico as well, making the trip to the United States less costly. This early migration was not as substantial as the earlier migrations from Europe had been, but it laid the foundation for further Mexican migration.[13] Moreover, the number of Mexican migrants to the United States was quite large relative to the population of Mexico. By 1930, persons in the United States who had been born in Mexico equalled almost 4 percent of the total population of Mexico and 0.5 percent of the population of the United States. However, during the next decade, the period of the Great Depression, the flow of immigration between Mexico and the United States reversed due to lack of jobs in the United States and provisions of U.S. immigration law that allowed deportation of legal immigrants who could not support themselves. By 1940, the number of Mexican-born persons in the United States was little more than one-half the number who had lived in the United States in 1930 and equalled less than 2 percent of the population of Mexico. During and after World War II, net Mexican migration to the

United States resumed and then accelerated. By 1980, more than 2 million Mexican-born persons lived in the United States. These persons constituted about 1 percent of the total U.S. population and equalled 3 percent of the population of Mexico. The tremendous population growth in Mexico between 1930 and 1980 explains why Mexicans in the United States were a smaller proportion of the total population of Mexico in 1980 than in 1930.[14]

MIGRATION WITHIN THE UNITED STATES

The U.S. decennial census reports migration in two ways. One question asks place of residence 5 years earlier and if it has changed, whether the change was within the same county, to another county within the same state, or to another state. The census also asks state of birth, in order to obtain estimates of lifetime migration. Annual data on internal migration are available only since 1947–1948. Approximately 16 to 20 percent of the total population has moved each year, about 6 percent have changed their county of residence, and about 3 percent have moved to a new state.[15] Fragmentary data suggest that rates of internal migration prior to 1947–1948 were essentially of the same magnitude as they have been since that date.[16]

There have been two important migration flow patterns in the United States. The first is the urban–rural or metropolitan–nonmetropolitan flow. Traditionally, the net flow of migrants tends to be away from rural or nonmetropolitan areas to urban or metropolitan areas. One of the first such large-scale rural–urban migrations within the United States was the movement of southern rural African-Americans to northern cities, beginning with World War I, as the flow of European migrants to U.S. cities waned. Like international migration, this internal migration slowed during the Depression years of the 1930s but regained momentum during World War II, when manufacturing employment opportunities for African-Americans increased, and continued into the 1960s.[17]

In every decade of the twentieth century, up to 1970, metropolitan areas have grown faster than nonmetropolitan areas, primarily because of migration. Between the 1970 and 1980 census years, nonmetropolitan areas grew faster than metropolitan areas, a turnaround of the long-term trend. The turnaround actually began before 1970 and continued through the 1970s, with nonmetropolitan relative growth peaking around 1975. Between 1980 and 1988, metropolitan growth again outdistanced that of nonmetropolitan growth. One important feature of the 1970s nonmetropolitan turnaround that persisted through the 1980s is deconcentration within nonmetropolitan areas. During the 1970s, the population of nonmetropolitan counties became less concentrated; that is, the outlying areas grew faster than the largest towns. This trend continued through the 1980s, even as nonmetropolitan growth slowed relative to metropolitan growth.[18]

The second major internal migration flow in the United States is from the northern and eastern regions of the country to the southern and western regions. With each decade since 1790, the *center of population* has moved progressively west, and in the twentieth century it also began moving south as well.[19] While

African-Americans had been moving away from the South since the end of the Civil War, this pattern reversed during the 1970s.[20]

The U.S. suburbanization patterns of the 1950s and 1960s typically involved white families leaving the central city for suburbs. With African-Americans leaving the rural South for central cities, metropolitan areas increasingly comprised central cities with high proportions of African-Americans and largely white suburbs. During the 1970s and 1980s, African-Americans, Hispanics, and Asians began to migrate to suburbs, with the result that the suburbs became more ethnically diverse.[21]

THEORIES AND DETERMINANTS OF MIGRATION

Traditional migration theory is based on push and pull factors related to the points of origin and destination, respectively. Potential migrants face one set of factors pushing them away from their current residence and another set of factors pulling them toward a new destination. In addition, potential migrants consider factors that intervene between their place of origin and possible destination. This kind of theory assumes that individuals weigh the costs of moving and staying against the benefits, using the push and pull factors, as well as the intervening factors, to estimate the costs and benefits.[22]

Historically, one of the most significant push factors has been the persecution of religious, racial, and political minority groups. Examples include the Puritan settlement of New England, the Jewish migration to Israel, the movement of African-Americans out of the South, and the aforementioned interchange of Moslem and Hindu populations between India and Pakistan.

Several economic variables may be considered push or pull factors. Relatively low wages may push individuals from one place, while higher wages may pull them to another place, if the wage differential is large enough to compensate for the costs of moving and adjusting to the new locale. As capital is introduced into an agricultural society as a substitute for labor, workers are displaced; these workers then move to places where they can find jobs. In Third World societies, therefore, economic development (at least in initial stages) may serve as a push, rather than a pull, factor. A further nuance of these two economic variables is that both individuals and families may be more highly motivated to minimize risks than to maximize wages.[23]

Laws restricting international migration are a major impediment to such movement. Nevertheless, there are many undocumented immigrants in countries throughout the world. Major destinations of undocumented immigrants include not only the United States but also Argentina, Venezuela, Hong Kong, and Saudi Arabia.[24] Undocumented immigrants flow from relatively poor nations to richer nations. Because the population growth rates of the world's poorer nations are so much higher than those of the wealthier nations, we can expect pressures for illegal immigration to continue to increase in forthcoming years.

In Chapter 2 we discussed how the attraction of an urban area may no longer reflect the factors that originally led to its establishment. Extending this perspective to migration in general, once a migration flow has been established (often for economic reasons), it may perpetuate for social reasons. Migrants form networks of relatives and friends, linking the place of origin to multiple destinations. One important function of these migrant networks is that they reduce the costs of moving and adjusting. Once a network has been established, subsequent migrants can rely on the previous movers for job contacts, temporary housing, and general information about life in the new location. As the network expands and the costs of migration decline even further, the migration flow continues to increase even if the original economic factors have lost some of their salience.[25] The social networks have reduced the costs of the intervening obstacles.

Desire for more adequate housing or a more favorable climate are two important pull factors that affect migration streams. The large numbers of immigrants to Sunbelt states and to suburban locations reflect these pull factors.

Not all individuals or families are equally likely to migrate. Age is the major differential in migration rates. The highest rates of mobility and migration are for young adults, but there is a secondary peak among young children. The reason for two peaks is that frequently the migrating unit is a young married couple with small children. In the United States in 1987, about 35 percent of all persons 20 to 24 years old had changed their residence during the previous year, and 13 percent had moved across a county line. Among children 1 to 4 years old, one-fourth had moved in the previous year, 9 percent to a different county. Moving rates declined by age, to 5 percent for persons 65 years old and over. Moving rates for men were less than 1 percentage point greater than those for women.[26]

Traditionally, when migration flows were based on differential economic conditions, young men were the first to move, although marriage, another factor influencing migration, usually results in women moving more than men. In some societies, rules of exogamy (marrying someone outside of one's family or social community) require individuals to marry someone from another village. In China, for example, women traditionally left their their own families to marry a man in another village and moved to live with his family.

CONSEQUENCES OF MIGRATION

Migration has consequences for the persons who migrate, the place of out-migration, and the place of in-migration. The larger social structure encompassing areas of both out-migration and in-migration also faces migration consequences. Net out-migration may have several important consequences for an area. It may relieve population pressure, as the large-scale migrations to North and South American did for Europe. With fewer surplus persons at the place of origin, the average level of wages may rise. In other settings, however, net out-migration may cause the value of land and real estate to decline. Moreover, areas of net out-migration suffer the loss of investments made to raise and educate children who then spend their productive years elsewhere. Since migration rates are selective by age, areas of net out-migration often have few young adults relative to the number of children and aged persons. Certain of these areas may also lose their most intelligent or best-educated persons in addition to their most rebellious and nonconforming elements.

Net in-migration may also have important consequences. If the area is underpopulated, the population increase may help the area to achieve economies of scale (reduction in the cost of goods because of increases in the scale of production and of marketing) and thus raise the general standard of living. Under other circumstances, net in-migration may result in some decline in average wage and salary income. In either case, a net flow of in-migrants will tend to raise the price of land and real estate.

Generally, areas with large numbers of in-migrants have a rather high proportion of young adults. They will also tend to have a rather heterogeneous population, since the migrants often come from diverse cultural backgrounds. As a result, areas with large in-migration are often more tolerant of new ideas. It is also possible, however, that a high rate of in-migration fosters social disorganization, or *anomie*. Elizabeth Bott's concepts of *open* and *closed social networks* are useful tools in understanding this hypothesis.[27] In a closed network, a high proportion of a given person's acquaintances know one another; in an open network this is not so. Thus group solidarity is presumed to be much higher when networks are closed. In her sample of urban English families, Bott showed that individuals who had recently moved into a community tended to have open networks, while the community's old-timers had closed networks. It is also plausible to presume that open networks are more common among non-migrants in areas of heavy in-migration than in other types of areas simply because many of one's neighbors are often new. Migrants, however, often develop their own closed networks through relocating to ethnic enclaves within urban areas.

For the social system comprising the areas of both net inflow and net outflow, the direct effect of migration, of course, promotes population redistribution. If migrants have responded to differences in job opportunities, this redistribution will further the economic development of the total system. The shift tends to increase the homogeneity of the various subregions in several respects. Since migrants tend to move from low-income areas to high-income areas, regional income inequalities lessen. Moreover, migration often helps to reduce regional disparities in other population characteristics as well. The migration of African-Americans away from the South before the 1980s made the regions of the United States less disparate in racial composition and brought the issue of race relations to a wider spectrum of the country. Migration may also be diluting the Catholic and Jewish concentrations in the northeastern states and the Protestant predominance in the South and West, creating greater similarity between these regions in modes of interreligious accommodations.

At the same time as migrants are moving within the United States, new foreign immigrants enter the country in particular places, thus continuing to foster regional variations in ethnic diversity. After a migration flow becomes established, it perpetuates itself as migrant networks develop. For example, in the mid 1980s, Filipinos were 6.8 times more likely to go to Hawaii than to the rest of the country. Mexicans are more than twice as likely to settle in Los Angeles, while Miami has large proportions of Cuban immigrants.[28]

NOTES

1. Bury, B., *The Invasion of Europe by the Barbarians* (London: Macmillan, 1928); Huntington, Ellsworth, *Civilization and Climate* (New Haven, CT: Yale University Press, 1924); Teggart, Frederick J., *Rome and China: A Study of Correlations in Historical Events* (Berkeley: University of California Press, 1939).
2. United Nations, Department of Social Affairs, *The Determinants and Consequences of Population Trends* (New York: United Nations, 1953), pp. 98–102.
3. U.S. Bureau of the Census, *A Century of Population Growth i.n the United States: 1790-1900*, by W. S. Rossiter (Washington, DC: U.S. Government Printing Office, 1909), p. 36; Taeuber, Conrad, and Irene B. Taeuber, *The Changing Population of the United States* (New York: John Wiley & Sons, 1958), p. 71.
4. Massey, Douglas, "The Social and Economic Origins of Immigration," *Annals of the American Academy of Political and Social Science*, 510 (July 1990), 60–72.
5. U.S. Bureau of the Census, *Historical Statistics of the United States: Colonial Times to 1957* (Washington, DC: U.S. Government Printing Office, 1960), pp. 56–59.
6. Calculated from data in U.S. Bureau of the Census, *Historical Statistics of the United States: Colonial Times to 1957*, p. 56; and United Nations, *The Determinants and Consequences of Population Trends*, pp. 11–13.
7. Edwards, R. Dudley, and T. Desmond Williams, eds., *The Great Famine* (New York: New York University Press, 1957), pp. 4, 388.
8. Massey, "The Social and Economic Origins of Immigration," pp. 60–72.
9. Bouscaren, Anthony T., *International Migrations Since 1945* (New York: Praeger, 1963), pp. 89-90; and *United Nations Demographic Yearbook, 1965* (New York: United Nations, 1966), p. 113.
10. Spate, H. K., *India and Pakistan: A General and Regional Geography* (New York: Dutton, 1957), p. 119.
11. Massey, "The Social and Economic Origins of Immigration," pp. 60–72.
12. Rubenstein, Richard L., *The Age of Triage: A Chilling History of Genocide from the Irish Famine to Vietnam's Boat People* (Boston: Beacon Press, 1983), pp. 188–189.
13. Massey, Douglas, "Economic Development and International Migration in Comparative Perspective," *Population and Development Review* 14, 3 (September 1988), 383–413.
14. Heer, David M., *Undocumented Mexicans in the United States* (New York: Cambridge University Press, 1990), pp. 24–31.
15. U.S. Bureau of the Census, "Geographical Mobility: March 1986 to March 1987," *Current Population Reports*, series P-20, no. 430 (April 1989); U.S. Bureau of the Census, *Current Population Reports*, series P-20, no. 235 (April 1972).
16. Lee, Everett S., "Internal Migration and Population Redistribution in the United States," in *Population: The Vital Revolution*, ed. Ronald Freedman (New York: Doubleday, 1964), p. 127.
17. Muller, Thomas, and Thomas J. Espenshade, with Donald Manson, et al., *The Fourth Wave: California's Newest Immigrants* (Washington, DC: The Urban Institute Press, 1985), pp. 11–12.
18. Long, Larry, and Diana DeAre, "U.S. Population Redistribution: A Perspective on the Nonmetropolitan Turnaround," *Population and Development Review*, 14, 3 (September 1988), 433–450; and Frey, William H., "Metropolitan America: Beyond the Transition," *Population Bulletin*, 45, 2 (Washington, DC: Population Reference Bureau, July 1990).

19. U.S. Bureau of the Census, *Statistical Abstract of the United States 1990* (Washington, DC: U.S. Government Printing Office, 1990), p. 8, defines the "center of population" as "that point at which an imaginary flat, weightless, and rigid map of the United States would balance if weights of identical value were placed on it so that each weight represented the location of one person on the date of the census."
20. Muller and Espenshade, *The Fourth Wave*, p. 12
21. Frey, "Metropolitan America."
22. Lee, Everett S., "A Theory of Migration," *Demography*, 3, 1 (February 1966), 47–57.
23. Massey, "The Social and Economic Origins of Immigration," pp. 60–72.
24. United Nations, Department of International Economic and Social Affairs, *International Migration Policies and Programmes: A World Survey* (New York: United Nations, 1982), pp. 68–81.
25. Massey, "The Social and Economic Origins of Immigration," pp. 60–72
26. U.S. Bureau of the Census, "Geographical Mobility: March 1986 to March 1987," *Current Population Report*, series P-20, no. 430 (April 1989).
27. Bott, Elizabeth, *Family and Social Network* (London: Tavistock Publications, 1957).
28. Allen, James P., and Eugene J. Turner, "Where to Find the New Immigrants," *American Demographics*, 10, 9 (September 1988), 22–27.

CHAPTER 7
AGE-SEX
COMPOSITION

DETERMINANTS OF AGE–SEX COMPOSITION

A population's *age–sex composition*—that is, the number of males and females in each of its age groups—is determined by its past levels of fertility, mortality, and migration. As fertility levels fluctuate over time, they create birth cohorts of varying sizes that have an impact on the population's age structure for many years. As birth cohorts age, they are subject to the effects of mortality and migration, both of which vary considerably by age and sex. All three of the demographic processes affect the age and sex composition in predictable ways, although the resulting age and sex structures are far from uniform.

In all populations, the ratio of males to females varies by age because of three factors. The first is the *sex ratio at birth*—the number of male births per 100 female births. For most populations, the sex ratio at birth is around 105 male births per 100 female births, and it usually falls between 104 and 107.[1] When values are significantly higher, it usually indicates unreported female births, female infanticide, or, more recently, selective abortions of female fetuses. The sex ratio at birth reached 111 in China during the 1986–1987 period. While all three of these factors may have contributed to this anomaly, the most significant one is that parents are concealing the births of female children in order to be allowed the chance to try again for a son.[2] (Chapter 9 provides further information regarding the Chinese One-Child Policy). The second contributing factor is the population's age and sex specific mortality rates. Because in most populations, male mortality is higher than female mortality, the sex ratio tends to decrease with age. Heavy military losses can appear in a population's age–sex pyramid for almost 50 years. For the United States in 1985, there were 98.4 males for every 100 females in the 25-to-49 age group, but for the 80-and-over age group, this ratio was only 46.8.[3] Differential male and female migration patterns can also affect the sex ratio at various ages.

When fertility, mortality, and migration rates remain relatively constant over time, a *stable age structure* emerges. The population pyramid retains the same shape, but it may expand or contract with population growth or decline. A special type of stable population is the *stationary population*, which results from constant vital rates and zero population growth. Most analyses of stable populations and stationary populations examine the effects of fertility and mortality only in a closed population—one with zero migration. The planet Earth is one example of a closed population. While international migration affects the age and sex structure of the United States, for most countries, fertility and mortality predominate by far over migration.

If we begin with a closed population that has experienced constant fertility and constant mortality for many years, we can observe a stable age structure that corresponds to that set of vital rates. If fertility and mortality fall, as in the demographic transition, the population age structure will change. Initially, as mortality declines, the age structure becomes younger, as the initial mortality declines favor younger ages. It is only when fertility declines that the population becomes older, as the number of children falls proportionately.[4] This conclusion varies with intuitive popular thinking. It is commonly assumed that populations with low mortality should have a high proportion of elderly persons and that populations with high mortality should have a low proportion of persons in the older age group. Instead, it is the difference in *fertility* rather than in mortality that is the chief cause of difference in age structure.[5]

Examining the age structures of stable populations under different fertility and mortality schedules helps to unravel the effect of the demographic transition on a population age structure. Figure 7–1 shows population pyramids corresponding to the demographic changes a society undergoes as mortality and fertility decline. Population A is a pretransition society with high mortality and high fertility. It has a young age structure with relatively more younger persons and fewer older persons. Population B illustrates the effect of lowering the mortality of population A and holding fertility constant. A comparison of populations A and B demonstrates how lower mortality creates a younger population. Note that the base of population B is wider and that the pyramid is steeper as age increases. Population C is a post-transition population, with mortality levels equivalent to population B and fertility such that the population is stationary (zero rate of natural increase). It is obvious from a visual inspection that population C is much older than either population A or population B, demonstrating that declining fertility has a larger effect than declining mortality in aging a population.

The age structures of actual populations, unlike those derived from model populations, tend to have irregularities, reflecting sharp temporary variations in the birth rate or sharp temporary changes in death or migration rates for particular age–sex groups. The age–sex composition of the Soviet Union in January 1959 is shown in Figure 7–2. Two notable features of this graph are the small number of

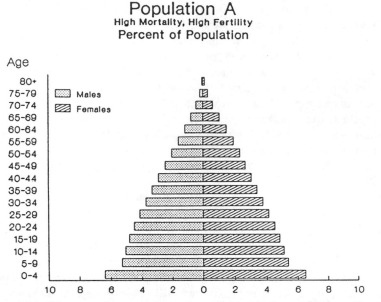

Population A
High Mortality, High Fertility
Percent of Population

Figure 7–1. Population age and sex structures at three stages of the demographic transition. Source: Calculated from Coale, Ansley J., and Paul Demeny, with Barbara Vaughan, *Regional Model Life Tables and Stable Populations*, 2nd ed. (New York: Academic Press, 1983), pp. 43, 75, 100.

Figure 7-1. Continued.

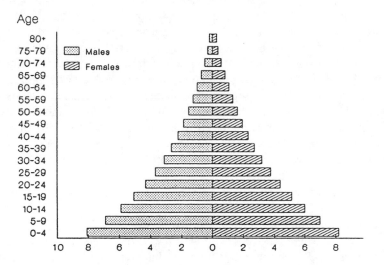

Population B
Low Mortality, High Fertility
Percent of Population

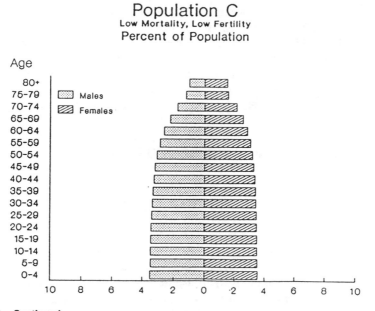

Population C
Low Mortality, Low Fertility
Percent of Population

Figure 7-1. Continued.

Figure 7–2. Age–Sex structures of the Soviet Union, January 1959. Source: Brackett, James W., "Projections of the Population of the USSR, by Age and Sex, 1964–1985," *International Population Reports*, U.S. Bureau of the Census, series P-91, no. 13 (Washington, DC: U.S. Government Printing Office, 1964), pp. 42–44.

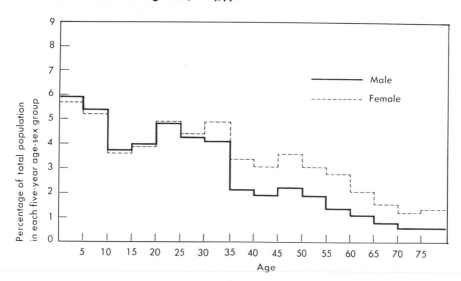

persons of both sexes 10 to 19 years old, and the very large deficit of males relative to females at ages 30 and over. The small proportion of persons 10 to 19 years old was largely the result of the reduction in the birth rate during World War II, when most men were serving in the military and were therefore separated from their wives. The extreme deficit of men at age 30 and over in the Soviet Union resulted from the large losses of military men during World War I, the Civil War of 1917 to 1921, and World War II, and of the severe repression that occurred during the Stalinist era.

CONSEQUENCES OF AGE–SEX COMPOSITION

Because age and sex arguably are the two most important determinants of human behavior, variations in age–sex structure may have various economic, demographic, and political consequences for the society in which they occur.

As the age structure of a society changes, so does its *dependency ratio*, the ratio of persons in dependent ages to persons in economically productive ages. Although the terms *dependent ages* and *economically productive ages* can have various bounds, the definition we will use here is that the dependent ages are the ages under 15 years and those ages 65 and over; the remaining age groups are considered economically productive. Of course, not all persons in the dependent years are economically unproductive; some are in the labor force and others contribute to household production outside of the labor force. Similarly, some persons between ages 15 and 65 are not economically productive—most notably those in school. The dependency ratio will change when the proportional size of any of the three components changes. For example, when mortality falls and a population initially becomes younger, the dependency ratio will rise because there are proportionately more children. Declining fertility lowers the dependency ratio because it lowers the proportional size of the child population. However, over time, lower fertility and, finally, lower mortality cause the proportional size of the older population to increase. As a typical country goes through its demographic transition, the dependency ratio tends to rise at first, then fall, and then rise again. In general, populations with high mortality and high fertility tend to have somewhat higher dependency ratios than populations with low mortality and low fertility. As a demographic measure, the dependency ratio is not particularly sensitive to changes in the age structure that result from lower mortality and fertility because as a population ages, the younger ages tend to decline and the older ages tend to increase proportionally. Since both are in the numerator of the dependency ratio, the changes offset each other.

It is also important to distinguish youth dependency from old-age dependency because of the different needs of each age group. Societies with large proportions of children need to spend relatively large amounts of money on education; societies with larger proportions of older persons need to spend more on health care. As the proportion of children in the U.S. population fell in the 1970s, so did school enrollments. Changes in the age composition of a population may lead to changes in the age patterns of consumption, however. One way that colleges and universities dealt with the possibility of declining enrollments as the baby-boom cohorts moved out of the traditional college ages was to encourage enrollment among persons of nontraditional college ages—women who had left school because of marriage or childbearing, retired persons who had never had an opportunity to attend college, and others who wanted to attend college either to improve their employment prospects or just to improve their minds.

Another economic consequence of changing age structures relates to the average age of the labor force. In a high-fertility population, the average age of the labor force is relatively young; however, as fertility falls, the average age of the labor force increases. A younger labor force generally requires lower wages and tends to be more flexible, as younger workers may be more willing to change jobs and move to new locations. An older labor force, however, is more responsible and experienced. Furthermore, job performance and productivity do not decline with age, and older workers do not show higher rates of absenteeism.[6]

An irregular age structure, usually caused by swings in fertility rates, may also have consequences with respect to the supply of labor, which will influence the wage and salary rate for particular age groups. For example, in the early 1950s in the United States there were relatively few persons 20 to 29 years old, and starting salaries of persons in this age group entering the labor force were exceptionally high. According to economist Richard Easterlin, small cohorts, such as this one, tend to face favorable economic conditions throughout their lives, while large cohorts, such as those born during and after the peak years of the baby boom, face less favorable economic conditions throughout their lives.[7] Because small cohorts have economic advantages, they tend to have higher fertility. The highest fertility rates of any cohorts born in this century are those of women born during the 1930s. Conversely, the large baby-boom cohorts have experienced lower fertility, as well as later marriage and increased labor force participation of married women in order to counterbalance their economic disadvantage.

While Easterlin points out the economic advantages of being born into a small birth cohort, Samuel Preston argues that small cohorts wield less political power, particularly in the childhood years.[8] Preston demonstrates that contrary to expectations, the baby-bust cohort received an education that was inferior to that of the baby-boom cohorts, as measured in terms of lower teachers' salaries and lower college-entrance test scores of persons entering U.S. teacher-training programs. Large cohorts benefit socially, as well, because their presence as a whole demands attention. The United States was decidedly youth oriented in the 1960s, but as the baby-boom cohort has aged, advertising has increasingly directed its messages toward progressively older persons.

Variation in age structure can also have consequences for measuring demographic processes. In particular, as noted in Chapter 3, a young population will tend to have a lower crude death rate than an old population, even if the age-specific mortality rates for the two populations are identical. Similarly, the crude birth rate will be affected by an abnormal sex ratio or by an unusually large or small proportion of persons of reproductive age. The small cohort born in China between 1959 and 1961, a period of famine in that country, was partially responsible for the decrease in the crude birth rate during the mid 1980s.[9] Migration rates are also affected by a population's age and sex structure. In particular, since young adults tend to be more mobile than middle-aged or older persons, a young population tends to have a higher migration rate than does an older one.

The probabilities of marriage for men and women also depend on the age and sex structure. If women usually marry men who are a few years older than themselves, then they will have more difficulty finding mates in a young population because there will be more women aged x-n years than men aged x. In societies with a young population and high mortality, a high proportion of women can marry only because a large number of men who have been widowed or divorced remarry women who have never married. In such a society, a large proportion of widows and divorced women will not be able to remarry. The excess loss of men in war can cause additional shortages of men for marriage. An imbalance in the ratio of men to women of marriable age is called a *marriage squeeze*. Due to the fluctuations in the U.S. birth rate during the 1930s and 1940s, there was a shortage of women in the early 1950s; however, by the late 1950s and through the 1960s, women faced a shortage of men. David M. Heer and Amyra Grossbard-Shechtman argue that this marriage squeeze for women, coupled with advances in contraceptive technology, led to lower proportions of women in traditional housewife roles and increasing proportions of women enrolled in colleges who were preparing to support themselves as an alternative to traditional marriage.[10]

Variations in the proportions of marriageable men to marriageable women also lead to variations in extramarital fertility. In particular, wars that markedly reduce the sex ratio at young ages often cause a substantial rise in births to unmarried women, which was the case for countries that suffered large military losses in World War II.[11]

Differences in age structure may even affect the relative power of liberals and conservatives within a nation. While some argue that individuals grow more conservative with age, there is also evidence that political affiliation takes shape early in early adulthood and persists throughout life. For this reason, it would be more correct to say that the changing cohort structure of a population has political consequences.[12]

Until recently, many writers, including demographers, dreaded the consequences of population aging. As long as fertility and mortality do not increase, populations around the world will continue to age, until they reach an equilibrium comparable to that of the population C we observed earlier. Most people would agree that increasing mortality is not an acceptable means to reverse the trend of population aging. Increasing fertility may be just as undesirable, even if it were possible, because the result would be a baby boom, which, as the experience of the United States has shown, requires tremendous accommodation from social institutions, like hospitals, schools, prisons, and the economy. Rather than attempting to change the inevitable outcome of population aging, societies must respond with significant changes in social structure and social roles.[13]

NOTES

1. Shryock, Henry, and Jacob Siegel, *The Methods and Materials of Demography*, condensed ed., by Edward G. Stockwell (New York: Academic Press, 1976), p. 109.
2. Hull, Terence H., "Recent Trends in Sex Ratios at Birth in China," *Population and Development Review*, 16, 1 (March 1990), 63–83.
3. Torrey, Barbara Boyle, Kevin Kinsella, Cynthia M. Taeuber, "An Aging World," U.S. Bureau of the Census, *International Population Reports*, series P-95, no. 78 (Washington, DC: U.S. Government Printing Office, September 1987).
4. Myers, George C., "Demography of Aging," in *Handbook of Aging and the Social Sciences*, eds. R. Binstock and L. George (New York: Van Nostrand, 1990), pp. 19–44; Grigsby, Jill S., "Paths for Future Population Aging," *The Gerontologist*, 31, 2 (April 1991), 195-203.
5. Coale, Ansley J., "How a Population Ages or Grows Younger," in *Population: The Vital Revolution*, ed. R. Freedman (New York: Doubleday, 1964) p. 47-58.
6. Harris, Diana, *Sociology of Aging*, 2nd ed. (New York: Harper & Row, Publishers, 1990), p. 267.
7. Easterlin, Richard A., *Birth and Fortune: The Impact of Numbers on Personal Welfare* (New York: Basic Books, 1980); and Easterlin, Richard, Christine Macdonald, and Diane J. Macunovich, "Retirement Prospects of the Baby Boom Generation," *The Gerontologist*, 30, 6 (December, 1990), 776–783.
8. Preston, Samuel, "Children and the Elderly: Divergent Paths for America's Dependents," *Demography*, 21, 4 (November 1984), 435–457.
9. Feeney, Griffith, et al., "Recent Fertility Dynamics in China: Results from the 1987 One Percent Population Survey," *Population and Development Review*, 15, 2 (June 1989), 297–322.
10. Heer, David M., and Amyra Grossbard-Shechtman, "The Impact of the Female Marriage Squeeze and the Contraceptive Revolution on Sex Roles and the Women's Liberation Movement in the United States, 1960 to 1975," *Journal of Marriage and the Family*, 43, 1 (February 1981), 49–65.
11. Heer, David M., *After Nuclear Attack: A Demographic Inquiry* (New York: Praeger, 1965), pp. 384–388.
12. Harris, *Sociology of Aging*, pp. 287–289.
13. Grigsby, "Paths for Future Population Aging" 195–203.

CHAPTER 8
POPULATION AND ECONOMIC DEVELOPMENT

From the time of Malthus, many economists and other social scientists have believed that rapid population growth impedes economic development. In their book *Population Growth and Economic Development in Low-Income Countries*, Ansley J. Coale and Edgar M. Hoover presented a model indicating that a 50 percent decline in fertility would significantly increase per capita income.[1] The field of economics, however, has recognized the positive as well as negative effects of population growth and acknowledges that the economic effects of population growth can vary from one setting to another. A perspective arguing against strong negative effects of population growth on economic development prevailed in the findings of the 1986 report by the National Academy of Sciences (NAS), *Population Growth and Economic Development: Policy Questions*, in contrast to an earlier National Academy of Science report published in 1971.[2]

In this chapter we will discuss the role of population growth in stimulating and retarding economic development. We will focus our discussion on the developing nations. However, we will also consider the effect of population growth rates on economic growth in the more developed countries, particularly those situations in which population growth can exert influences in opposite directions, depending on the context. We will examine the effects of population growth on a country's economic development, looking specifically at (1) economies of scale, (2) marginal returns, (3) changes in the dependency ratio, (4) savings and capital formation, (5) per capita investment in education and health, (6) per capita income, and (7) income inequality. An overview of national economic conditions around the world will provide a backdrop to this discussion.

INCOME AND RESOURCE INEQUALITY AMONG NATIONS

A great gulf currently divides the nations with low-income economies from those with high-income economies. The high-income nations, with a total population of only 777 million, had an average per capita gross national product (GNP) of $14,430 in 1987. The low-income nations, with a total population of 2.8 billion, had a per capita GNP of only $290. During the 1980s, a group of formerly less developed nations improved their economic well-being, thus bringing about a third economic category of nations, those with middle-income economies. In 1987 this middle group had a combined population of 1.0 billion and an average GNP of $1,810. By the late 1980s, the low-income nations included China, India, Nigeria, and Indonesia. The lower-middle–income group comprised Senegal, Bolivia, Egypt, Nicaragua, and Turkey among others, while the upper-middle–income group included Brazil, Hungary, Argentina, the Republic of Korea, and Greece. The high-income nations included those in Western Europe, North America, Australia, New Zealand, and the oil-producing countries, such as Kuwait and the United Arab Emirates. The per capita GNP of the United States was more than 100 times that of Ethiopia and about 60 times that of either India or China, illustrating the extreme gap between the high-income and low-income nations.[3]

With respect to per capita resources, the more developed nations currently hold a large advantage. The United States in 1985 produced almost 50 times as much electricity per capita as China, and almost twice as much as the Soviet Union and Japan.[4]

Because of modern means of communication and transportation, the low- and middle-income nations are now more aware than ever of the economic prosperity of the wealthier nations. This awareness has incited the people and governments of the low- and middle-income nations to expect rapid economic development.

POPULATION GROWTH AND ECONOMIES OF SCALE

As far back as 1776, Adam Smith discussed *economies of scale*—how the cost of production could be reduced by increasing its size. Henry Ford demonstrated Adam Smith's principles by offering his Model T Ford at a price considerably lower than that charged by his competitors, who did not use mass-production techniques. If population growth, by expanding the market for goods, allows for an increase in the scale of production, and if an increase in scale reduces average productive costs, then population increase will bring about lower production costs. For example, it is quite possible that the past increases in the population of the United States made possible certain economies of scale in American productive and service industries, particularly in railroad transportation and heavy industry. Australia and a few other nations with low population density might achieve lower average costs through the economies of scale that further increases in population could make possible. There is probably an optimum scale of production, however, and increasing the scale of operations beyond a certain point results in higher rather than lower average costs. For example, the streets of many American cities are now so overcrowded with vehicles that the average costs of transport operations within cities would decline with a decrease rather than an increase in the scale of vehicular movement.

A burgeoning population is not the only means by which business operations can achieve escalation. International trade also holds great potential, since a large international market may offer as many opportunities for economies of scale as a large internal market. Moreover, the internal market for all but the most necessary goods and services will increase as much through a rise in the nation's per capita income as by an increase in the number of consumers.

The 1986 NAS report examined the effect of slower population growth on agricultural and industrial economies. The report found that economies of scale exist in both urban and rural settings; however, population density has a different effect on each. For manufacturing, economies of scale require only a medium-sized city, and further population density does not bring additional economic advantages. While urban density is related to economies of scale, national population density does not affect economies of scale, nor does it stimulate manufacturing innovations. Increased population density, can, however, allow agricultural economies to take advantage of technological innovations. Irrigation and transportation systems, for example, require a critical level of population density for feasibility.[5] Because economies of scale rely on high ratios of capital to labor, which Third World countries generally do not possess, these countries may have difficulty taking advantage of scale effects.[6]

POPULATION GROWTH AND DIMINISHING MARGINAL RETURNS

The detrimental effect of population growth on the average cost of production is that every increase in population results in a diminution of natural resources per capita. Malthus first brought this point to the attention of the Western world, followed by David Ricardo, a nineteenth-century English economist. Both men developed what is called the *law of diminishing marginal returns*. Their discussion revolved around the two factors of production: land and labor. Land, they argued, was a fixed factor, since the amount of land could in only small degree be altered through human intervention. Labor, on the other hand, was a variable factor, since each increase in population would result in an increase in the size of the labor force. The interest of the classical economists lay in (1) the total amount of food that could be produced on a given piece of land, depending on the amount of labor that was applied, and (2) the marginal increment in production that could be achieved by applying an additional unit of labor. According to their theory, at the beginning, when the first few units of labor are applied, the marginal returns increase; that is, each successive unit of labor adds more units of product than its predecessor. Thus the classical economists recognized the economies of scale. However, beyond a certain point, they argued, further applications of labor would earn successively less additional product, until finally an additional unit of labor would result in no marginal return at all.

Malthus contended that the world of his time was subject to diminishing marginal returns from additional increments of labor, and that any increase in population would result in a decline in economic production per capita. That Malthus was proven wrong in his prediction of a declining living standard was the result of the unforeseen advances in technology that have taken place since his time. As population increases, lands that were previously thought insufficiently productive are brought into use, minerals and fuels that were earlier thought to be too inaccessible or of insufficiently high quality are extracted, and more units of labor are applied to each unit of land or other resources. This perspective places less emphasis on natural resources and instead argues that human population growth and well-being depend more upon materials that people themselves construct; hence, population growth may not be harmful to economic development and under some circumstances can actually be helpful.[7]

Unless advances in technology continue to surpass population, however, living standards are bound to decline once the population exceeds a certain critical size. The exact size of population beyond which diminishing returns set in and the exact relation between each increment in population size and each increment in production depend on a multitude of factors. China is the most recent nation of significance to examine optimum population size through a systems analysis taking into account natural resources, production inputs, levels of pollution, and standard of living. This kind of analysis led the Chinese government to implement a strong birth-planning policy, which will be discussed in Chapter 10.[8]

POPULATION GROWTH AND THE DEPENDENCY RATIO

In the previous chapter we discussed how different patterns of fertility and mortality produce differences in the dependency ratio. We pointed out that in stable populations, high fertility has a major influence in creating an elevated dependency ratio, and low mortality has a minor influence. Stable populations with high fertility and low mortality therefore have the highest ratio of dependent to productive age groups.

Coale and Hoover demonstrated how changes in fertility and mortality might affect the ratio of nonearning dependents to earners in India. According to their projection, which assumed declining mortality but no change in fertility, the ratio of dependents to wage earners would rise from 1.51 in 1956 (the actual figure) to 1.71 in 1986. They carried out another projection with the same mortality decline, but with a 50 percent decline in fertility by 1981, in which the ratio of dependents to wage earners instead decreased to 1.24 by 1986.[9] It is clear from these figures that the standard of living in the average Indian family would have improved greatly if such a reduction in fertility had occurred, whereas a continued decline in mortality might have threatened existing living standards merely by increasing the number of persons dependent on each wage earner.

POPULATION GROWTH, SAVINGS, AND CAPITAL FORMATION

Coale and Hoover completed their work by considering how their projected 50 percent decline in fertility might affect (1) the total amount of capital investment, (2) the proportion of total capital investment applicable to improving productivity rather than providing for population increase, and (3) resultant increase in income per equivalent adult consumer.[10] They assumed that 30 percent of any increase in income per equivalent adult consumer would be invested. They also assumed that investments made merely to maintain the existing level of equipment per capita of an expanding population would not serve to raise total production—a reasonable assumption, since during the period of their projection the size of the labor force was not materially affected by fertility reduction. They did not assume any declining returns caused by increasing scarcity of natural resources per capita.

According to Coale and Hoover, in the population with declining fertility, income per equivalent adult consumer would gradually increase relative to that in the population with unchanging fertility. After 10 years (that is, in 1966), average income per consumer in the population with declining fertility would be only 3 percent higher than that in the population without fertility change. By 1976, however, it would be 14 percent higher, and by 1986, 41 percent higher. Assuming fertility reduction, income per consumer would be 95 percent higher in 1986 that it had been in 1956; assuming no fertility reduction, it would be only 38 percent higher.[11] The actual demographic and economic trends in India between 1956 and 1986 came close to mirroring Coale and Hoover's projections that assumed no change in fertility.[12] Coale and Hoover's work clearly demonstrated that fertility reduction might have a substantial effect on the future course of economic development in India and other low-income nations.

Some subsequent critics have challenged Coale and Hoover's model of how fertility regulation would affect savings. They have argued that large families may not necessarily have lower levels of savings. Children may contribute to household income or spur their parents to work more.[13] The 1986 NAS report concluded that for the less developed nations, slower population growth would increase the ratio of capital to labor. An increase in this ratio would in turn increase the level of per capita output "though theory and limited empirical evidence suggest that this effect may be relatively modest."[14] Other scholars have disagreed with the 1986 NAS report. For example, Lester Brown has argued that national accounting systems purporting to measure gross national product "miss entirely the environmental debts the world is incurring."[15]

POPULATION GROWTH AND PER CAPITA INVESTMENT IN EDUCATION AND HEALTH

Slowing population growth invariably results from a large-scale fertility decline, with a shift from larger families to smaller families. The 1986 NAS report concluded, based on a review of numerous studies, that children in large families have poorer health and less education than children from small families, primarily because larger families have less to spend per child on schooling, food, and medical services. The report went on to argue that family planning can increase the level of health and education through two mechanisms. First, individual families will have fewer children, and therefore each child will have more resources. Second, if family planning is subsidized, then presumably, the proportion of births to poorer families will decline. At a macro level, the 1986 NAS report found that school enrollments are not lower in low-income countries, but that such countries spend less per student and have larger class sizes.[16]

POPULATION GROWTH AND PER CAPITA INCOME

Until the 1980s, many economists assumed that rapid population growth led to lower per capita income, primarily through lowering the ratio of capital to labor, making workers less productive. However, cross-national studies have repeatedly failed to show a clear relationship, either positive or negative, between population growth and per capita income when examining these two variables for many countries in a given year. One possible reason for this lack of correlation is that a reciprocal relationship exists between population growth and per capita income. Not only does population growth affect per capita income, but there may also be some causation in the other direction as well.[17] In particular, if per capita income increases, the death rate may fall, and the population growth rate will increase. Coale has shown that high fertility, not rapid population growth, is associated with low per capita income.[18]

POPULATION GROWTH AND INCOME INEQUALITY

The 1986 NAS report concluded that slower population growth tended to decrease income inequality by both class and sex, assuming that large families impart economic disadvantages to parents and especially to children. As noted in Chapter 5, one of the prerequisites of a fertility decline is that the population perceives small families to be relatively advantageous, economically and otherwise. Without subsidized family planning, however, poor persons may not be able to afford the means to control their fertility, and they therefore continue to suffer the economic disadvantages of larger families. If government-sponsored family-planning programs allow the poor to control their fertility, then income inequality will decline. In the longer term, as the population growth rate falls, wages tend to rise, thus increasing the incomes of workers relative to those of capitalists. Because, as the NAS committee noted, women bear more of the burden of child rearing, reducing fertility, particularly unwanted fertility, would reduce economic inequality by sex as well as by class.[19]

NOTES

1. Coale, Ansley J., and Edgar M. Hoover, *Population Growth and Economic Development in Low-Income Countries* (Princeton, NJ: Princeton University Press, 1958).
2. National Academy of Sciences, *Population Growth and Economic Development: Policy Questions* (Washington, DC: National Academy Press, 1986); National Academy of Sciences, *Rapid Population Growth: Consequences and Policy Implications* (Baltimore: Johns Hopkins University Press, 1971).
3. The World Bank, *World Development Report 1989* (New York: Oxford University Press, 1989), pp. 164–165.
4. Calculated from The Economist, *The World in Figures: Editorial Information Compiled by The Economist* (Boston: G. K. Hall & Co. 1988), p. 32.
5. National Academy of Sciences, *Population Growth and Economic Development*, pp. 47–52.
6. Kelley, Allen C., "Economic Consequences of Population Change in the Third World," *Journal of Economic Literature*, 26 (December 1988), 1685–1728.
7. Simon, Julian L., *The Ultimate Resource* (Princeton, NJ: Princeton University Press, 1981); and Preston, Samuel H., "Are the Economic Consequences of Population Growth a Sound Basis for Population Policy?" in *World Population and U.S. Policy: The Choices Ahead*, ed. Jane Menken (New York: W. W. Norton & Company, 1986), pp. 67–95.
8. Song, Jian, and Jingyuan Yu, *Population System Control* (New York: Springer-Verlag, 1988).
9. Coale and Hoover, *Population Growth and Economic Development*, pp. 25, 235.
10. In calculating the number of equivalent adult consumers, males 10 and over were given a weight of 1, children under 10 a weight of 0.5, and females 10 and over a weight of 0.9.
11. Coale and Hoover, *Population Growth and Economic Development*, p. 280.
12. Menken, Jane, "Introduction," in *World Population and U.S. Policy: The Choices Ahead*, ed. Jane Menken (New York: W. W. Norton & Company, 1986), p. 15.
13. Kelley, "Economic Consequences of Population Change in the Third World," pp. 1685–1728.
14. National Academy of Sciences, *Population Growth and Economic Development*, pp. 40–46. Quote from p. 46.
15. Brown, Lester, "The New World Order," in *State of the World 1991: A Worldwatch Institute Report on Progress Toward a Sustainable Society* (New York: W. W. Norton & Company, 1991), p. 8.
16. National Academy of Sciences, *Population Growth and Economic Development*, p. 53–61.
17. Kelley, "Economic Consequences of Population Change in the Third World," pp. 1685–1728.
18. Coale, Ansley J., "Population Trends and Economic Development," in *World Population and U.S. Policy*, ed. Menken, pp. 96–104.
19. National Academy of Sciences, *Population Growth and Economic Development*, pp. 62–65.

CHAPTER 9
POPULATION AND POLITICAL POWER

The *political power* of a nation or group is its ability to influence other nations or groups to engage in behaviors or enact policies that they would not otherwise engage in or enact. This power may be exercised by (1) providing rewards for compliance with one's goals, (2) threatening the use of force for failure to comply, or (3) actually using force when compliance has not otherwise been induced. Population variables influence the relative power both of nations in international politics and of groups engaged in political conflict within a nation. However, the influence of population variables on power is not always clear. In particular, it would be wrong to postulate that an increase in population size necessarily leads to greater political power.

POPULATION AND POWER IN INTERNATIONAL AFFAIRS

Although there is without question a positive correlation between the size of a nation's population and its relative influence in international affairs, the correlation is only a rough one. Certainly none of the nations with very small populations is a great power, and the two most politically powerful nations in the world, the Soviet Union and the United States, are exceeded in population by China and India. Perhaps the most striking recent illustration of the imperfect correlation between population size and power in international affairs was the 1967 victory of Israel, with a population of only about 2.5 million, over its Arab opponents, whose combined population totaled about 100 million.

Clearly, population size alone cannot explain variation in international power. Other important variables that contribute to a nation's force in world affairs include income per capita, the possession of natural resources specifically necessary for warfare, the degree of government motivation to achieve international goals, and the efficiency of the government in mobilizing resources to attain these goals.[1]

Population size is important for two reasons. First, a large population is necessary if a nation is to have a large military. The largest militaries in the world are in the Soviet Union, China, the United States, and India, which also happen to have the largest populations, although not in the same order.[2] Second, population size is important because a large labor force can produce enough surplus to pay for the cost of a military establishment, foreign aid, and any other expenditures that enhance the international power or influence of a nation. If the surplus amount is constant for each member of the labor force, then the effort to maintain or increase the nation's power will vary directly with the size of the labor force. Moreover, the larger the population, the larger the labor force, and hence the potential resources available for increasing the nation's power will vary directly with the size of the population.

The amount of surplus extracted from each member of the labor force and devoted to aggrandizing the nation's power may not, however, be constant, because income per capita varies among nations and is thus another important variable in determining national power. The higher the per capita income, the lower the proportion of all income that the worker must spend on the absolute necessities of life. Hence the proportion of each individual's income that can be spent to increase the power of the nation will vary directly with the level of per capita income.

In addition to a large population and high per capita income, a nation will have greater military power if it posesses natural resources such as petroleum, coal, and iron ore, which are necessary for maintaining a military establishment. Finally, powerful nations possess great motivation to achieve international influence and are able to mobilize resources efficiently to attain these goals. Iraq, with a relatively small population of 16 million in 1986, was able to muster a military 40 percent as large as that of the United States.[3]

Table 9–1 shows the 12 nations that have the largest populations, the highest per capita gross national product (GNP), the highest total GNP, and the greatest total production of steel (a measure of productive capacity). It is apparent from this table that population size, per capita GNP, and steel production are not closely correlated, as only three countries—the United States, Japan, and Germany—appear on every list, and only two additional countries—the Soviet Union and China—are on two of the lists. Population size serves primarily as a proxy measure of potential military force and labor force. A substantial population appears to be a necessary but not sufficient prerequisite for attaining world power; witness the fact that India, Indonesia, Brazil, and Nigeria, all nations with large populations, do not have particularly high per capita GNPs nor high levels of steel production. Per capita GNP appears to be less important than population size, as it is possible for relatively small countries to achieve high levels of economic development without wielding international influence.

Table 9-1. The Twelve Nations with Largest Population, Highest Per Capita Gross National Product (GNP), Highest Total GNP, and Greatest Steel Production, circa 1990

NATION	1990 POPULATION (IN MILL.)	NATION	1987 PER-CAPITA GNP	NATION	1987 TOTAL GNP (IN BILL.)	NATION	1987 STEEL PRODUCTION (IN MILLION METRIC TONS)
China	1,120	Switzerland	27,300	United States	4,527	USSR	147.9
India	853	Japan	19,410	USSR	2,460	Japan	110.2
USSR	291	United States	18,570	Japan	2,369	United States	101.5
United States	251	Sweden	18,490	West Germany	1,126	West Germany	43.3
Indonesia	189	West Germany	18,450	France	868	China	37.1
Brazil	150	France	15,620	Italy	746	Italy	26.3
Japan	124	Canada	15,550	United Kingdom	667	France	22.8
Nigeria	119	Austria	15,440	China	471	Poland	18.0
Bangladesh	115	Netherlands	14,590	Canada	402	Canada	15.7
Pakistan	115	Belgium	13,940	Brazil	291	Czechoslovakia	15.2
Mexico	89	Italy	13,010	Spain	284	Romania	12.4
Germany	80	East Germany	11,860	Poland	260	Spain	12.4

Sources: Population: Population Reference Bureau, *1990 World Population Data Sheet* (Washington, DC: Population Reference Bureau, 1990); *Per capita GNP, total GNP (in 1987 U.S. dollars) and steel production:* U.S. Bureau of the Census, *Statistical Abstract of the United States, 1990* (Washington, DC: U.S. Government Printing Office, 1990), pp. 840, 851.

Of these indicators of national power, total GNP and aggregate steel production have the greatest validity. Total GNP, of course, is the product of population and per capita GNP. Likewise, a high level of steel production is possible when both population and per capita GNP are high. Moreover, the level of steel production depends on government motivation in favor of international power, since a sizable steel industry is a prerequisite for large-scale armaments manufacture. Nevertheless, Japan, the nation with the second-highest aggregate steel production, does not have a large military force. The five nations with the greatest total GNPs were the United States, the Soviet Union, Japan, West Germany, and France. In terms of total steel production, the Soviet Union led the world in 1987, followed by Japan and the United States. Further back were West Germany and China.

If population size and political power are not highly correlated, it follows that a nation that wishes to increase its power relative to other nations should not necessarily encourage an acceleration of its population growth. There are two reasons that an acceleration of population growth may not augment a nation's power. First, an increased growth rate made possible by an increase in fertility can produce additional military personnel only after a lag of some 20 years following the increase in the birth rate. Second, a high rate of population growth may be detrimental to a nation's ability to raise its per capita income. For already densely populated nations such as China, India, Bangladesh, Pakistan, and Indonesia, where the level of per capita income is extremely low, a better strategy for increasing national power may be to reduce fertility in order to facilitate an increase in per capita income, given the caveats of Chapter 8. Less densely settled nations, such as the United States, with very high per capita income, might suffer a decline in power if their populations were to decline relative to those of other nations.

POPULATION AND INTRANATIONAL POWER

Population size and distribution influence the U.S. political process as mandated in the Constitution. The U.S. Census, taken once each decade, endeavors to count every person residing in the United States, regardless of citizenship or voting status. The resulting population counts dictate how many Congressional representatives each state receives, according to the Constitution. All states have at least one representative, and they acquire more representatives as population size increases. Every 10 years, therefore, some states lose representatives, while other states gain them, but the total number of representatives remains fixed.[4] Furthermore, every 10 years, states draw new boundaries for Congressional districts to take into account changes in population size and distribution within the state. Revenue sharing, whereby the federal government allocates money to states, cities, and other localities, also relies on population counts. Because of the high stakes associated with acquiring representatives and federal money, the U.S. Census has been subjected to close scrutiny, particularly by localities concerned about undercounts. Because minority populations in urban areas are the ones most likely to be undercounted, cities and states with large cities have voiced the most dissatisfaction with the quality of U.S. Census results. In a lawsuit brought by New York City and the state of New York against the U.S. Census Bureau in which they asked that the bureau adjust the 1980 Census for undercount, a federal court decided in favor of the bureau, declaring that it did not have to adjust for undercount.[5] The bureau does not intend to adjust the 1990 census either, although New York has brought another lawsuit, this time seeking adjustment to the 1990 census.

Besides affecting representation and fund allocation, population also influences other political behaviors—voting and leadership. In a democracy, in which one person has one vote, it follows that groups with large populations would have more power. In the United States, groups defined by ethnicity, age, birth cohort, social class, gender, and geography have been identified as political contingents. Such groups can increase their political power by increasing either their size or their level of participation.

Because voting in the United States is done by secret ballot, we can obtain information about voters only indirectly, through surveys. The largest such survey, carried out by the U.S. Bureau of the Census, is the November supplement to the Current Population Survey, which asks individuals about their voting behavior. As expected, the survey tends to overestimate the proportion of persons who voted in the November election, as voting is a socially desirable behavior and some respondents are reluctant to admit that they did not vote. For example, 57 percent of respondents ages 18 and older reported voting in the 1988 presidential election, even though the tabulated votes indicated that only 50 percent of the eligible population voted. The percentage of eligible persons who vote has dropped steadily since 1964, when 69 percent of the voting age population reported voting.[6]

Social and economic characteristics relate closely to voting and voter registration behavior. Age is a particularly strong determinant of voting. Whereas only 36 percent of persons 18 to 24 years old voted in 1988, 69 percent of persons 65 years and older voted. Political participation among older persons has increased slightly from the 1960s, while it has fallen dramatically among those 18 to 44. One explanation for the change among older persons is the increase in educational attainment among more recent birth cohorts of older persons, since education is also strongly related to voting behavior. In 1988, more than three-fourths of college graduates reported voting, whereas slightly more than one-third of persons with an elementary education reported voting. Similarly, voting proportions increased with income. Whites report higher voter turnout (59 percent) than either African-Americans (52 percent) or Latinos (29 percent), although one reason for the low levels of voting among Latinos is that one-third of them were not eligible to vote in the 1988 election because they were not citizens. Women were slightly more likely than men to report voting (58 percent versus 56 percent).[7]

One important question is the extent to which social and economic groups vote as a bloc. African-Americans, Puerto Ricans, and Mexican-Americans tend to vote with the Democratic party, while Cuban-Americans generally align themselves with Republicans. Social class also influences party identification, as persons with higher incomes tend to vote Republican, and those with lower incomes tend to vote

Democratic. Ethnicity and class both appear to be more salient determinants than either age or gender. Even though women tend to have somewhat more liberal attitudes on certain political issues, they are not a strong voting coalition. Similarly, politicians have not been able to count on a "senior vote" or a "baby-boom vote."[8]

Even though the voting population reflects considerable diversity, the ethnic and sex composition of elected leaders has not changed accordingly. Only one-fifth of elected officials across the country are women, with African-Americans and Latinos comprising 2 percent and 1 percent, respectively. Growing numbers of women and minority-group members have entered politics at the state and local levels during the 1970s and 1980s.

The distribution of domestic political power faces other nations besides the United States. In the Soviet Union, policies that attempt to limit the fertility of Muslim women coexist with pronatalist policies for other women, in response to concern over growing numbers of the Soviet Muslim population. The non-Russian Soviet republics have attempted to control the in-migration of Russians, in order to preserve their culture and maximize political authority, while the European republics have taken steps toward "greater Russianization."[9]

NOTES

1. This framework closely follows the thinking in Davis, Kingsley, "The Demographic Foundations of National Power," in *Freedom and Control in Modern Society*, eds. Morroe Berger et al. (New York: Van Nostrand, 1954), pp. 205–243; and Organski, Katherine, and A. F. K. Organski, *Population and World Power* (New York: Alfred A. Knopf, 1961).
2. *The World Almanac and Book of Facts 1990* (New York: World Almanac), p. 791.
3. *The World Almanac and Book of Facts 1990*, p. 791.
4. For a succinct explanation of the Congressional allocation formula, see Poston, Dudley, "Apportioning U.S. Congress: A Primer," *Population Today*, 18, 7/8 (July–August 1990), 6–10.
5. Haupt, Arthur, "New York Loses Census Case," *Population Today*, 16, 1 (January 1988), 4.
6. U.S. Bureau of the Census, "Voting and Registration in the Election of November 1988," *Current Population Reports*, series P-20, no. 440 (Washington, DC: U.S. Government Printing Office, October 1989).
7. U.S. Bureau of the Census, "Voting and Registration in the Election of November 1988."
8. O'Hare, William P., and Carol J. De Vita, "America in the 21st Century: Governance and Politics," (Washington, DC: Population Reference Bureau, 1990).
9. Anderson, Barbara A., and Brian D. Silver, "Growth and Diversity of the Population of the Soviet Union," *The Annals of the American Academy of Political and Social Science*, 510 (July 1990), 155–177.

CHAPTER 10
POPULATION LEGISLATION AND POLICY

Change in population size, geographic distribution, composition, and process may all be influenced by government decrees and legislation. Some of the legislation affecting population is intentionally designed to influence one or more aspects of a nation's population. However, much of the legislation affecting population has some other goal as its primary aim. Only the former can be called population policy, but we cannot neglect the latter, since its total effect on population may be even greater than that of the legislation consciously designed to have an impact on population.

The ultimate effect of population legislation may be on size, geographic distribution, or composition. The mechanism to achieve any one of these effects is a change in one of the three population processes: mortality, fertility, and migration. Any legislation affecting a population process will of course have an impact on the rate of change in population size. In addition, laws that induce change in mortality, fertility, or migration differentials will also affect population distribution and composition. It will therefore be convenient to divide our discussion of legislation according to whether there is an attempt to influence mortality, fertility, or migration.

POLICIES AFFECTING MORTALITY

In his analysis of controlling population growth, Malthus pointed to the positive checks—war, famine, and disease—as likely restraints. These "miseries" have plagued human societies from the beginning of their history, and one major task of leaders is to ensure the health and safety of their people. Although governments generally value the preservation of human life, they have other values to consider, and these sometimes take precedence over the alleviation of human suffering. There are even examples in human history of deliberate genocidal policies, such as Hitler's against the European Jews.

Almost all governments place the independence of the nation above the protection of human life, and many have also considered imperial aggrandizement to be a higher value. As a result, throughout human history, wars and armed conflict have resulted in millions of deaths not only of soldiers, but of civilians as well. However, the inhumanity of war led nations to attempt to control its outbreak through the mechanism of international organizations. The first such organization, the League of Nations, was not successful in preventing World War II—mainly because it was not taken seriously by many of its member nations, and partly because the United States refused to join it. The second international organization, the United Nations, has enjoyed a qualified success. Since its inception following World War II, it has been able to help stave off encounters among various great powers but has failed to prevent a rash of smaller but serious conflicts.

One of the first recorded efforts to deal with famine is found in the biblical story of Joseph, son of Jacob, who interpreted the Egyptian pharoah's dream as predicting 7 years of famine following 7 years of plenty. The Pharoah put Joseph in charge of storing food for the famine, a task that he carried out successfully. Throughout history, famines have threatened isolated human settlements and entire nations. More recently, a major famine in China in around 1960 was the consequence of environmental disasters (like droughts and floods) and, more importantly, flawed public policy. Local leaders kept giving optimistic, but false, harvest reports to their superiors because of the tremendous pressure to make the Great Leap Forward a success. By the time national leaders learned of the widespread famine, it was too late to distribute food effectively to the areas in need. Furthermore, because China at that time had poor international relations, particularly with the United States and its allies, the Chinese were unwilling to ask for help, and in turn other countries were reluctant to send food to China.[1]

While modern medical institutions have developed elaborate systems of public health and medical care, even in preindustrial times governments were concerned about disease prevention. Even without understanding the germ theory of disease, people have been aware of the contagious aspect of many diseases, and governments have instituted quarantines, although in the case of the fourteenth-century plague, quarantine measures failed because the disease was spread by fleas and rats.[2]

Since the inception of industrialization, almost all nations have attempted to reduce mortality among their own people by means of public health programs. Inoculation against infectious disease, clean water supplies, sewage systems, and the regulation of food and drugs are measures that cost relatively little money yet have had a great impact on mortality reduction. More recently, public health measures have included medical research, which the United States has funded through the National Institutes of Health.

Government provision of health care began as part of general social insurance programs in western European countries. In these nations, either the government establishes medical clinics that provide the public with largely free care, or it subsidizes the cost of patients' medical and hospital bills. Some countries provide coverage for 100 percent of the population (for example, Scandinavia and Great Britain), while others exclude as many as 10 to 15 percent of the population through eligibility criteria. In Japan, 99 percent of all workers and their dependents are fully or partially covered by a national insurance program that dates back to 1921. New Zealand began providing comprehensive health care for its entire population in 1939, and Australia's healthcare program, which began with coverage of prescription drugs, eventually encompassed physician and hospital bills as well. Even some developing countries—for example, Chile, Brazil, Peru, Iran, and Turkey—have instituted healthcare services, although they are not as comprehensive in terms of population coverage as those of other countries.[3]

Unlike most of the other developed nations, the United States does not have a general government program of free or subsidized medical care. Nevertheless, the federal government has gradually been assuming more and more responsibility in this area. Since 1946, the federal government has subsidized the construction of hospitals, and in 1965 Congress passed an amendment to the Social Security Act that greatly expanded federal participation in medical-care programs. Medicare pays for part of the hospital and medical expenses of all persons 65 years and over, with the federal government directly reimbursing patients or health providers. Somewhat ironically, Medicare does not cover long-term care, even though 36 to 45 percent of persons who reached age 65 in 1990 could expect to spend some time in a nursing home.[4] In contrast, Medicaid, part of federal legislation, is implemented at the state level of government. Medicaid requires each state, with the help of federal financing, to provide free medical care for persons in poverty, as established by a means test. Because Medicare is implemented by the federal government, older persons living in one state do not receive different levels of health care from that program compared with persons living in another state. However, with Medicaid, poor persons living in one state may receive fewer benefits than those living in another state.

Government expenditures on health programs have had several effects on differential mortality. Public health and preventive medical care in general help to reduce death rates among infants and children more than among older adults. Not surprisingly, developed countries with national health programs have lower infant mortality rates than those in the United States. Sometimes, however, health policy can benefit older ages disproportionately. Samuel Preston demonstrated that between 1968 and 1980, mortality improvements were greatest among persons aged 65 and over, which he attributed in part to Medicare entitlements.[5] When healthcare programs equalize access to medical services, then social-class mortality differentials will decline. Since poor persons generally cannot afford adequate medical care, government programs of medical care probably do more to reduce death rates among the poor than among the well-to-do. Recall from Chapter 3 that the primary reason for the high infant mortality rates in the United States relative to other developed nations is the high rate of infant mortality among nonwhites, who tend to have disproportionately high levels of poverty. Finally, all governments must make choices about which programs to fund and how much funding one program receives over another. These decisions tend to be made in a political context and may not rely consistently on rational scientific evidence to guide the legislative and appropriations process. As healthcare spending escalates and becomes an increasing proportion of the national economy, governments have considered the possibility of rationing healthcare services, even among those who can pay for them. Great Britain has already implemented rationing policies, particularly for expensive diagnostic and treatment techniques.[6]

Many government policies that have resulted in the extermination of human life have not been explicitly legislated, but rather happen in the implementation process. One exception is capital punishment, which explicitly decrees that society can take a human life when an extremely heinous crime (usually murder) has been committed. Examples of government genocide, however, often began as policies to deal with "surplus populations." When less extreme solutions, such as forced migrations or withholding food and medical help, did not work, then some governments resorted to outright murder. One of the best-known examples of mass execution is the Holocaust, during World War II, when Hitler exterminated most of the European Jewish population.[7]

POLICIES AFFECTING FERTILITY

Pronatalist Policies

Legislation with a conscious attempt to influence fertility has a long history, and until recent times almost all of it was pronatalist, since the only control humans had over high mortality rates was to develop elaborate social norms and institutions to keep fertility rates high. Most traditional religions have pronatalist rules encouraging large numbers of children and restricting sexual activity to procreation within legitimate family units. Political institutions have also developed pronatalist laws. The Code of Hammurabi, enacted in Babylon in the twentieth century B.C., is the first recorded attempt to elevate fertility by means of legislation.[8] Pronatalist policies were also enacted in Rome during the reign of Caesar Augustus, sometime between 18 B.C. and A.D. 9. The *Lex Papia et Poppaea*, for instance, contained various provisions designed to encourage marriage and the raising of children: Fathers were given preference in public office according to the number of children in the family, and mothers of large families were given the right to wear distinctive clothes and ornaments. The main intent of the laws was to encourage births, not in the general population, but rather among the aristocrats, who apparently were not reproducing themselves in numbers sufficient to please the government. However, the aristocrats chose not to let the government order their conjugal behavior, and the laws proved both unenforceable and ineffectual. They were abolished entirely when Christianity, which placed a higher value on celibacy than on marriage, became the religion of Rome.[9]

Pronatalist legislation was also enacted in France and in Spain during the seventeenth century. In Spain, men who married early or who had a large family received partial or full exemption from taxes. The French legislation was similar to the Spanish, but provided in addition that any of the nobility who had ten or more living legitimate children were henceforth to receive annual pensions. There is some doubt, however, as to whether the Spanish legislation was ever put into effect, and the French legislation was soon repealed.[10] The seventeenth-century Spanish and French pronatalist policies had been established because the government feared the military consequences of, in the case of Spain, an absolute loss in population, and in the case of France, a loss relative to population in other nations. In Spain, the population had declined from about 10 million in 1500 to about 6 million in 1700.[11]

During the eighteenth and early nineteenth centuries, the actual increase in European population largely stilled the demands for pronatalist legislation. Pronatalist sentiment revived in many European nations coincident with the fertility decline of the late nineteenth and early twentieth centuries. Pronatalist legislation has probably been carried to its fullest extent in France, where, as previously mentioned, defeat by Prussia during the war of 1870 and the terrible losses of World War I caused the government to resolve that the French birth rate should match that of Germany. But such legislation has been important at one time or another in almost all of the European nations.

One of the principal components of modern pronatalist legislation in France and other nations has been programs of family allowances, whereby parents receive monetary payments on behalf of their children without regard to individual financial need. The French family allowance system evolved gradually. Beginning in 1918, family allowance schemes were voluntarily organized by various industries; each company within the industry contributed to an industrywide equalization fund, which in turn distributed the family allowance payments. Legislation in 1932 nationalized the system of family allowance payments, and according to the new French law, all industrial employees were to be given cash allowances for each dependent child. In 1939 the French system was further enlarged to include workers in all occupations.[12]

An increase in the birth rate was also the main object of family programs introduced into Germany by Hitler, into Italy by Mussolini, and into the Soviet Union by Stalin. In the Soviet Union a munificent program for families with three or more children was enacted in 1944. This legislation closely followed the staggering population losses that the nation had suffered during the first years of World War II. In 1948, however, the benefits were cut in half, and after that date the impact of the program was further diluted by the very substantial increase in the Soviet wage level. In 1944, the monthly payment to a family after the birth of the fifth child had been about 51 percent of the average wage, whereas in 1964 it was worth only 12 percent.[13]

In many of the European nations with family allowance programs, the main aim has been social welfare rather than population increase. Since the parents of large families often do not have enough income to provide adequately for their children, family allowance payments help to equalize the position of children from large families. Sweden, for example, instituted an extensive family allowance program along with other programs after the Swedish Population Commission of 1935 recommended steps to reverse the decline in fertility. The Swedish Population Commission believed that the fertility decline stemmed from families' inability to afford more children. Indeed, the underlying rationale for the entire set of policies was to increase, rather than restrict, reproductive freedom by allowing families to have the number of children they wanted.[14]

More recently, governments of developing countries have adopted family allowance schemes in order to keep fertility from declining, as they believe that a large population is necessary for international power. Saddam Hussein, who became president of Iraq in 1979, started a system of allowances and benefits, including 100 percent paid maternity leave for 10 weeks, in order to encourage all women to have at least four children.[15] Between 1967 and 1987, the total fertility rate in Singapore fell from 5.5 births to 1.6 births per woman, due to a comprehensive family-planning program. Since 1983, however, Singapore has attempted to reverse this downward trend in the birth rate. One of the unique features of Singapore's pronatalist policy is that it attempts to encourage highly educated women to have at least three births, and at the same time, it discourages fertility among poor women by paying them to be sterilized.[16]

Another tactic to raise fertility is to limit access to contraception and abortion. While the motivation for passing such legislation is often pronatalist, an important attitude sustaining such legislation is the belief that the widespread availability of contraception and abortion encourages sexual promiscuity (among women in particular). One example of restrictive birth control legislation was a French law enacted in 1920 that prescribed imprisonment for anyone engaging in birth control propaganda, divulging means of birth control, or facilitating use of methods to prevent pregnancy. An important loophole was that the condom could be legally sold only if the intent was protection from venereal disease.[17] In the United States, restrictive birth control legislation was in effect in Connecticut and Massachusetts as late as 1965 and 1966. Since 1966, the distribution of contraceptive information and the sale of contraceptive devices have been legal throughout the nation. The main intent of legalizing contraception in the United States was not to manipulate the fertility rate, but instead to increase reproductive freedom and protect individual privacy.

Until the 1800s, Western governments did not legislate prohibitions against abortion. Local courts, when faced with abortion cases, used the principle of "quickening" to guide their decisions. British common law stipulated that before "quickening," the time when the pregnant woman begins to sense fetal movement, usually by the fourth or fifth month of gestation, the state had no say in the matter because the fetus was not considered a human life. In the United States, legislation prohibiting abortion under certain circumstances appeared first in Connecticut in 1821, followed by ten other states or territories over the next 20 years, although most of this legislation still applied to abortions that occurred after quickening. By the mid 1800s, when abortions increased in number and became more publicly visible, new laws were enacted with the support of physicians, who were interested in women's health and wanted to professionalize the field of medicine by regulating the activities of midwives, the foremost providers of abortions. By 1900, practically every state had passed laws limiting abortion; these laws stood for over 60 years.[18]

Various U.S. state legislatures enacted liberalized abortion legislation in the late 1960s and early 1970s. Perhaps the most important of these changes occurred in New York, where abortion by a licensed physician was allowed on any grounds within the first 24 weeks of pregnancy.[19] In congruence with the shift in public opinion on this issue, the U.S. Supreme Court ruled on January 22, 1973, in *Roe* vs. *Wade*, that during the first trimester of pregnancy, the decision to have an abortion must be left solely to a woman and her physician. After the first trimester, the Court decreed that regulations "reasonably related to maternal health" were permissible (such as a regulation requiring that abortions be performed in a hospital). However, legislation prohibiting abortion was deemed constitutional only in the rare instances in which the fetus has capacity for life outside the mother's uterus and the abortion was not necessary to preserve the mother's physical or mental health.[20]

Subsequent Supreme Court decisions have regulated access to abortion for certain segments of society. The Court has allowed legislation restricting the use of Medicaid funds for abortions, thus limiting access to abortions for poor women. Another ruling allowed federal regulations to prohibit doctors in federally-funded clinics from informing their patients that abortion is an option. The Court has also allowed states to pass parental consent laws that require girls under the age of 18 to have the consent of one or both parents before they have an abortion. This ruling has affected the availability of abortion to teenagers.

After liberalizing their abortion laws in the 1950s, several eastern European nations adopted more conservative abortion policies in the 1960s and 1970s, not for religious or ethical reasons, but in response to the falling birth rate.[21] One of the most dramatic effects of this change came in Romania, where, without warning, the government restricted abortion in 1966. The general fertility rate rose from 62 births per 1000 women aged 15 to 44 in 1966-1967 to 140 per 1000 in 1967-1968. By the mid 1970s, fertility had almost returned to previous levels, as women turned to alternative forms of birth control, including illegal abortion.[22]

Most Asian countries have been able to liberalize abortion policies with less resistance than that faced by Western nations. In contrast to Asia, most governments in Africa and Muslim countries continue to have strict laws forbidding abortion because they have strong religious support.[23]

There are many laws in the United States and elsewhere, in addition to the ones reviewed here, that probably have pronatalist consequences even though their main intent is doubtless one of furthering welfare. In the United States perhaps the most significant pronatalist legislation is the federal income tax law. The law allows each taxpayer exemptions for dependent persons (usually children). The income tax laws of the various states also tend to favor family heads with children over other taxpayers.

Fertility Reduction Policies

Although legislation restricting fertility is of much more recent origin than its converse, within the last few years such legislation has assumed great importance in many areas of the world. An early example of antinatalist legislation was a decree passed in 1712 in Württemberg (now in Germany) prohibiting marriage unless ability to support a family could be proven.[24] Nevertheless, antinatalist legislation was of little general consequence until after World War II.

In the post–World War II period, Japan was the first nation to undertake seriously an antinatalist policy. Following the devastation of the war, living standards in Japan had fallen to 52 percent of the prewar average. Furthermore, Japan had been stripped of its territorial possessions in Asia, and as a result was forced to receive 6.6 million repatriates and demobilized soldiers from abroad. In 1949 the House of Representatives of the Japanese Diet expressed its official belief that means should be taken to reduce the birth rate. In the previous year Japan had legalized abortion for reasons of maternal health. In 1949, in accordance with the new antinatalist policy, legislation was enacted to allow abortion for economic reasons. In 1952, a further amendment to the law allowed abortion at the discretion of only one physician and authorized midwives and nurses to give guidance in contraception. As a result of these legal changes, the reported number of induced abortions increased greatly, from less than 250,000 per year in 1949 to annual totals of more than 1 million in 1953. Since 1955 the number of abortions has declined as the proportion of the population practicing contraception increased. Coincident with the legalization of abortion and the official encouragement of contraception, fertility in Japan declined dramatically. In 1947 the gross reproduction rate was 2.20, but since 1957, fertility has been close to or below replacement level.[25]

Beginning in the early 1960s, developing countries began to adopt family planning programs with the explicit intent of lowering the birth rate. Using funds from the United Nations, the World Bank, certain developed nations (most notably, the United States), private foundations, and their own resources, programs made contraception available to couples in order to help them have the number of children they desired, often targeting those who said they wanted no more children.[26]

In the late 1960s a sharp debate arose regarding the adequacy of family-planning programs alone to reduce worldwide birth rates to a sufficiently low level. Kingsley Davis argued that the real problem was not that unwanted births needed to be eliminated, but that persons were motivated to want too many children.[27] Davis further maintained that family planners, in implying that the only need was a perfect contraceptive, avoided discussion of the possibility that "fundamental changes in social organization" were necessary prerequisites of achieving lower fertility. The fundamental changes that Davis outlined were part of social and economic development. In a speech, President Lyndon Johnson declared that 1 dollar spent on family planning in a country with high fertility would bring more results than spending 20 dollars on development. In response, the demographer Etienne van de Walle remarked that 20 dollars spent on development would have a greater effect if 1 dollar were spent on family planning.[28]

As birth control became more widely available, and as social and economic development spread, fertility preferences started to change, and thus the demand for contraception increased further. In 1983, over 90 percent of the developing world's population lived in countries with family-planning programs. Countries that have both a strong family-planning program and vigorous social and economic development have experienced the greatest success in reducing the birth rate, but even in settings with only moderate development, family-planning programs have made considerable gains. Countries with relatively low levels of development, however, appear to have little success with family planning, even when the programs have considerable government support.[29]

The government of India, as early as 1952, adopted a national policy in favor of family planning, but little was actually done until the advent of India's Five Year Plan in 1961. The Indian government has made family planning a high priority since the mid 1960s. In 1967, only 4 percent of couples at risk of pregnancy were using contraception, but by 1987, 38 percent were using some form of birth control. Because India is such a large and culturally diverse country with modest socioeconomic development, it has been difficult to implement a successful family-planning program there. Furthermore, the central government has tried to run a program without understanding the needs of the workers and potential clients at the grass-roots level, which has led to unworkable policies. For example, family-planning workers were assigned unreasonably high quotas for gaining new acceptors, leading them to become discouraged and apathetic. In addition, the Indian family-planning program relied too heavily on one form of contraception, sterilization, which people were reluctant to accept because of its irreversibility. While the Indian family-planning program as a whole cannot be called an unqualified success, certain districts have increased contraceptive use to more than half of the population at risk, although the government has not yet been able to understand why some of these programs are successful while others have not met their goals.[30]

FAMILY PLANNING POLICY IN INDIA

Family-planning programs in smaller, more homogeneous countries have made considerable progress towards reducing fertility. An island-wide program in Taiwan with unofficial government backing began in 1964, following a local program conducted in the city of Taichung. Initially, the intrauterine device (IUD) was the only available contraceptive. The program, using funds from the U.S. Agency for International Development (USAID), provided physicians in private practice with IUDs and paid them about 75 cents for each insertion; the patient paid an additional 75 cents. In 1967 the government programs added oral pills, and in 1970 patients could also choose condoms. Field workers in each local community promoted family planning, and the mass media promoted contraception in a limited way. By 1972 more than half of the married women 15 to 44 years of age were estimated to be current users of contraception.[31] In 1963, the year before the program began, the total fertility rate in Taiwan was 5.4, but by 1971 it had declined to 3.7, and in 1990 it had fallen to 1.8.[32]

Undoubtedly, the most comprehensive and dramatic set of government policies designed to lower fertility have been implemented in the People's Republic of China. In the 1950s, after the 1949 revolution, the Chinese government began to consider large-scale human management, and as early as 1957, Mao Zedong discussed population size as a variable to include in long-term planning. The famine from 1959 to 1961, following the Great Leap Forward, led the Chinese to reconsider fertility control, and so the Chinese birth rate exceeded 35 per thousand from 1962 to 1966. In the late 1960s, family planning was limited to urban areas, with some educational efforts in rural areas, and the birth rate remained above 30 per thousand. Between 1970 and 1978, the Chinese government strengthened birth control efforts and changed their stance from planning for population growth to restraining growth, using the phrase "later, longer, fewer" to summarize the policies of later marriage, longer birth intervals, and fewer children. Two children was considered the optimum family size at this time. By 1978, the birth rate fell to 18 per thousand, a decline of almost 50 percent in less than a decade, but the Chinese government was worried about the momentum for large population growth inherent in the young age structure, due to the high fertility of the 1960s. In order for the country to reach its target of zero population growth by the year 2000, the government decided to implement the now well-known one-child family policy, and used a variety of incentives and what some call coercive measures to gain compliance.[33] The government decentralized the implementation of the policy, relying on authorities at the village level to keep births under control. In actuality, the one-child policy was most successful in urban areas, and by the late 1980s, most rural areas allowed a second child under certain conditions. In 1984 the central government explicitly prohibited coercive policies, although they denied ever condoning them.[34] Despite the Chinese government's attempts to equalize the preference for sons and daughters, some rural districts allowed couples with a daughter to have a second birth. Even though the goal of zero population growth by 2000 may not be met, the Chinese family-planning program represents one of the most impressive efforts to reduce fertility. The total fertility rate in rural areas fell from 6.3 children per woman in 1970 to 2.9 in 1980 and 2.45 by 1987, with a low of 2.27 in 1985.[35]

Fertility policies, when successful, have a major impact on the age composition of a nation. Pronatalist policies tend to produce a young population, and antinatalist policies an older one. Government programs to influence fertility can produce socioeconomic differences in fertility as well. Family allowance programs have their greatest impact among low-income groups, since the supplement for child-rearing awarded to low-income families is a comparatively higher proportion of their total family income. Restrictive laws concerning birth control and abortion also have their greatest effect in low-income groups, since married couples of high socioeconomic status can evade them more easily. Antinatalist programs that provide family-planning information and contraceptive devices can also have more of an effect on the lower socioeconomic strata, particularly if the cost of contraception in the private marketplace is relatively high.

POLICIES AFFECTING MIGRATION

Migration policy comprises a wide assortment of legislation and implementation practices. Laws concerning international migration usually cover immigration, as nations are usually more concerned about persons entering their borders than those leaving. Some countries completely forbid immigration, while others encourage it. Some countries have strict laws controlling emigration for their entire populations or for certain segments, such as men of military age. Other countries may not try to forbid people from leaving the country but instead do not allow them to take many assets out of the country. Although the laws of most nations concerning internal migration are generally permissive rather than either prohibitory or encouraging, certain governments have exercised vigorous control over internal migrants.

In the seventeenth and eighteenth centuries, a mercantilist ideology, which saw a large population as the key to national wealth and power, encouraged many of the governments of Europe to attempt to prohibit emigration and to encourage immigration. In the late seventeenth century, the French Minister Colbert enacted legislation prescribing the death penalty for persons attempting to emigrate or helping others to emigrate anywhere except to a French colony. In 1721 Prussia passed a similar law, and the Prussian Emperor Frederick the Great invested state funds to subsidize immigrant settlements. In Russia, both Tsar Peter and Tsarina Catherine subsidized colonists from abroad—mostly from Germany.[36]

The nineteenth century, influenced by the economic doctrines of *laissez faire*, was the great period of unrestricted international migration. During this century the European governments freely permitted emigration, and the newly independent United States of America accepted millions of immigrants. In the latter part of the nineteenth century, the United States began to restrict unlimited immigration, at first excluding criminals and prostitutes in an 1875 federal law, followed by subsequent legislation that barred other undesirable or deviant types, such as the mentally ill, mentally retarded people, alcoholics, and convicts. In 1882 Congress passed the Chinese Exclusion Act, making all Chinese ineligible for entry into the United States. By 1917 similar exclusions applied to all Asians.[37]

After World War I, governments again took a more active role in policy relating to international migration. Changes in U.S. immigration laws in 1921 and 1924 greatly restricted the number of immigrants to the United States, establishing a quota for each of the countries outside the Western Hemisphere. No numerical restrictions applied to immigrants from Mexico or other Latin American countries.

Each of the nations of northwestern Europe received a much larger quota relative to the potential number of immigrants than those of southern or eastern Europe. The justification for the quota differentials was the presumed ease with which immigrants from northwestern Europe could assimilate themselves.[38] During World War II, labor shortages led to a new type of immigration policy, the "temporary worker" program, to employ agricultural workers from workers, known as *braceros*. This initially insignificant program ultimately became the basis for large-scale immigration of undocumented workers.[39]

By the 1960s a changing climate of opinion with respect to the inferiority or superiority of different ethnic groups made it possible for President John F. Kennedy to advocate the abolition of the discriminatory national-origins quota system, and a law accomplishing this was enacted in 1965 under the Johnson administration. The 1965 law called for the abolition of the national-origins quota system as of July 1, 1968—but nevertheless imposed an overall annual quota of 170,000 immigrants from outside the Western Hemisphere and 120,000 from within it (exclusive of immediate relatives of U.S. citizens). This legislation granted preference to persons with relatives already in the United States, to persons with needed occupational skills, and to refugees.[40]

The 1965 law did not cover illegal immigration, and by the mid 1970s this issue led many members of Congress to push for new immigration legislation. Moreover, the growing number of political refugees from Southeast Asia and Latin America required the government to reformulate its refugee policy. Whereas the previous refugee law, passed in 1952 during the McCarthy era, required refugees to be fleeing from communism or from the Middle East, the new law broadened the definition of refugee to include persons who feared persecution on the basis of "race, religion, nationality, membership in a particular social group, or political opinion."[41]

In 1986 Congress passed the Immigration Reform and Control Act (IRCA), which contained two important and innovative (at least in the United States) components. First, federal law dictated employer sanctions for knowingly hiring illegal aliens, with fines for initial offenses and prison sentences for repeaters. Second, the law allowed aliens to apply for amnesty by May 4, 1988, if they were able to prove that they had lived in the United States since before January 1, 1982 and they did not have criminal records. Agricultural workers had to fulfill somewhat more lenient criteria.[42] Over 3 million persons applied for amnesty by the final deadline in 1988. IRCA also authorized an additional $400 million toward expanding the number of officers patrolling the southern border, a move that the Immigration and Naturalization Service (INS) claims to be successful, although critics disagree.[43]

Despite the passage of IRCA in 1986, members of Congress continued to insist on further immigration reform. After much debate, the Senate and the House of Representatives were able to agree on a comprehensive bill, the Immigration Act of 1990. While IRCA dealt primarily with illegal immigration, the 1990 law focused on legal immigration. The major provisions of this bill included, first, a ceiling of

700,000 immigrants annually between 1992 and 1994, and then a drop to at least 675,000 annually. The 700,000 cap, however, is not fixed, as immediate relatives of U.S. citizens can enter the country above this level, and so can refugees who comply with the 1980 Refugee Act. Second, immigrants were to enter in one of two categories—either as families or as independents. The bulk of immigrant visas would be granted to family members of U.S. citizens. Separate from families were independent immigrants, who compete for visas on the basis of a point system, with more points for potential immigrants who have desirable skills or large investment sums that would enable them to create jobs in the United States.[44]

Europe, which was primarily a region of emigration until the mid-twentieth century, began to suffer from labor shortages after World War II, a period of substantial economic growth. In response, the governments of individual countries implemented guestworker programs in the 1960s to recruit, transport, and host migrants on a temporary basis.[45] These policies resulted in rather large proportions of foreign-born persons in the western European populations by the early 1980s. Half of the countries had more than 4.5 percent foreign born residents, with France and Switzerland having 11.1 and 16.7, respectively. Because of restrictive policies subsequently implemented by countries in this region, immigration declined rapidly by the early 1980s. The United Nations recommended that individual governments protect the rights of migrant workers and respect the principle of family reunification.[46]

Internal migration does not tend to be regulated as closely as international migration. Population distribution policies with countrywide implications include controlling metropolitan growth, encouraging the growth of small towns and medium-size cities, and instituting rural development policies. Less comprehensive strategies include relocation of the national capital (as in the case of Brazil), new towns, land colonization, policies for border areas, and regional development schemes. China, for example, has a population distribution policy with the goal of developing small metropolitan areas by encouraging the growth of consumer-goods manufacturing.[47]

Although the United States has neither legislative restrictions on internal migration nor subsidies to encourage it, various types of government actions influence the flow of internal migrants. For example, a federal decision to grant a military contract to a particular corporation or to establish a military base in a particular location will influence the migratory flow. Area redevelopment programs for economically depressed areas attempt to mitigate out-migration from the area.

It should be obvious that migration policies address both qualitative and quantitative issues. All nations regulate the number of persons entering or leaving their borders, and many governments have sought to reduce ethnic heterogeneity by promoting immigration only among persons considered to be relatively similar in culture and racial composition. Countries may also attempt to raise the quality of their population by giving preference to immigrants with desirable skills. Clearly, nations want to control not only the total volume of migration, but also the type of individuals who come and go.

LIMITS TO POPULATION POLICY

Governments throughout the world are becoming more aware of the consequences of population processes and are increasingly contemplating and adapting population-influencing policies. The underlying conundrum facing policy makers, as Paul Demeny summarizes, "is that individual decisions with respect to demographic acts do not add up to a recognized common good...."[48] Ideally, policies that serve the interests of individuals also serve society at large. Human societies spent millenia developing norms, values, and ideologies that enabled populations to survive in the face of high mortality. The transition to lower fertility therefore requires massive changes in deep-seated beliefs. We are beginning to see, however, that it may be just as difficult to encourage couples to have enough children to replace themselves, once a "low fertility" culture takes hold. The demographic challenge for societies in the future, therefore, will be to develop population policies that serve both individual interests and the common good.

Furthermore, individual demographic acts tend to encompass behavior that most societies hold sacrosanct to some extent. Since its inception, the United Nations has maintained that reproductive freedom is a basic human right.[49] The "unalienable right" in the U.S. Declaration of Independence to "life, liberty, and the pursuit of happiness" can be interpreted to cover good health and residential freedom of choice. Fertility, mortality, and migration—aggregate-level processes—translate at the individual level to giving (or not giving) birth, dying (or surviving), and moving (or staying put). The effectiveness of population policies depends on the willingness and ability of governments to regulate these behaviors.[50]

For many, population policy is synonymous with fertility policy, and therefore, it is not surprising that of all population policies, those attempting to control fertility have received the greatest scrutiny by social scientists and other writers. To be acceptable to the United States and the United Nations (arguably the most significant funding sources), family-planning programs have had to be voluntary. There appears to be a naive assumption that if individuals have the freedom to make their own reproductive choices, the resulting outcome will be in the best interest of society. In a case study of population commissions in two democratic societies—one with too-high fertility and one with too-low fertility—both commissions said that the problem stemmed from the inability of couples to reproduce at their desired level. The solution in both cases was the same: increase individual reproductive freedom.[51] Because China's family-planning program was not completely voluntary, it received harsh criticism and lost United Nations funding. Even the central Chinese government itself could not condone coercive tactics. While the right to bear children seems to be fairly universal, its opposite, the right to choose not to give birth, has not received as much protection, as evidenced by the tremendous level of unintended childbearing throughout the world. The current demographic threat to human society is not high mortality, but high fertility. Once all societies have completed their demographic transitions, they will next have to deal with the likely problem of low fertility.

NOTES

1. Ashton, Basil, et al., "Famine in China, 1958–61," *Population and Development Review*, 10, 4 (December 1984), 613–645.
2. McNeill, William H., *Plagues and Peoples* (New York: Anchor Press, Doubleday, 1976), pp. 150–151.
3. Roemer, Milton I., *Comprehensive National Policies on Health Care* (New York: Dekker, 1977), pp. 38–40.
4. The Pepper Commission, U.S. Bipartisan Commission on Comprehensive Health Care, *A Call for Action* (Washington, DC: U.S. Government Printing Office, 1990), p. 11.
5. Preston, Samuel H., "Children and the Elderly: Divergent Paths for America's Dependents," *Demography*, 21, 4 (November 1984), 435–457.
6. Aaron, Henry, and William B. Schwartz, "Rationing Health Care: The Choice Before Us," *Science*, 247 (January 26, 1990), 418–422.
7. Rubenstein, Richard L., *The Age of Triage* (Boston: Beacon Press, 1983), pp. 128–164.
8. Glass, David V., *Population Policies and Movements in Europe* (Oxford: Clarendon Press, 1940), p. 86.
9. Ibid., pp. 86–90.
10. Ibid., pp. 91–95.
11. United Nations, Department of Social Affairs, *The Determinants and Consequences of Population Trends* (New York: United Nations, 1953), p. 9.
12. Glass, *Population Policies and Movements in Europe*, pp. 99–124.
13. Heer, David M., "Recent Developments in Soviet Population Policy," *Studies in Family Planning*, 3, 11 (November, 1972), 257–264.
14. Grigsby, Jill S., "Democratic Constraints on Demographic Policy," *Comparative Social Research*, 7 (1984), 387–396.
15. de Sherbinin, Alex, "Iraq," *Population Today*, 18, 10 (Washington, DC: Population Reference Bureau, October 1990), p. 12.
16. Palen, J. John, "Population Policy: Singapore," in *Population Policy: Contemporary Issues*, ed. Godfrey Roberts (New York: Praeger, 1990), pp. 167–178.
17. Glass, *Population Policies and Movements in Europe*, pp. 159-162; "Rapport sur la regulation de Naissances en France," *Population*, 21, 4 (July–August 1966), 647–648.
18. For a thorough history of abortion and abortion policy in the United States, see Mohr, James C., *Abortion in America: The Origins and Evolution of National Policy, 1800–1900* (New York: Oxford University Press, 1978); and Tietze, Christopher, Jaqueline Darroch Forrest, and Stanley K. Henshaw, "United States of America," in *International Handbook on Abortion*, ed. Paul Sachdev (New York: Greenwood Press, 1988), pp. 473–494.
19. Association for the Study of Abortion, *ASA Newsletter*, 5, 2 (Summer 1970), 2–4.
20. "United States Supreme Court Issues Sweeping Decision on Abortion," in *Family Planning/Population Reporter*, 2, 1 (February 1973), 1–5.
21. Sachdev, Paul, "Abortion Trends: An International Review," in *International Handbook on Abortion*, pp. 1–21.
22. Tietze, Christopher, and Stanley K. Henshaw, *Induced Abortion: A World Review 1986* (New York: Alan Guttmacher Institute, 1986), p. 132–133.
23. Sachdev, "Abortion Trends," pp. 1–21.
24. Glass, *Population Policies and Movements in Europe*, p. 98.
25. Muramatsu, Minoru, ed., *Japan's Experience in Family Planning—Past and Present* (Tokyo: Family Planning Federation of Japan, 1967), pp. 27, 69, 83–101.
26. Freedman, Ronald, "Family Planning Programs in the Third World," *The Annals of the American Academy of Political and Social Science*, 510 (July 1990), 33–43.

27. Davis, Kingsley, "Population Policy: Will Current Programs Succeed?", Science, 163 (November 10, 1967), 730–39.
28. Both remarks were paraphrased in Menken, Jane, "Introduction," in World Population and U.S. Policy: The Choices Ahead, ed. Jane Menken (New York: W. W. Norton & Company, 1986), pp. 23–24.
29. Freedman, "Family Planning Programs in the Third World," pp. 33–43.
30. Ibid.
31. Family Planning in Taiwan, Republic of China, 1965–66 (Taichung: Taiwan Population Studies Center, 1966); Johnson, Stanley, Life Without Birth (Boston: Little, Brown, & Company, 1970), pp. 68–92; and Keeny, S. M., ed., "East Asia Review, 1972" Studies in Family Planning vol. 4, no. 5, p. 119.
32. 1965 Taiwan Demographic Fact Book, Republic of China (Taipei: Department of Civil Affairs, Taiwan Provincial Government, 1966), pp. 226–227; 1971 Taiwan Demographic Fact Book, Republic of China (Taipei: Ministry of Interior, Republic of China, 1972), p. 501; Haub, Carl, Mary Medeiros Kent, and Machiko Yanagishita, "1990 World Population Data Sheet" (Washington, DC: Population Reference Bureau, 1990).
33. Banister, Judith, China's Changing Population (Stanford, CA: Stanford University Press, 1987).
34. Greenhalgh, Susan, "Shifts in China's Population Policy, 1984–86: Views from the Central, Provincial, and Local Levels," Population and Development Review, 12, 3 (September 1986), 491–515.
35. Kane, Penny, The Second Billion: Population and Family Planning in China (Ringwood, Australia: Penguin Books, 1987), pp. 46–102, provides an overview of Chinese family planning policies. For more recent information, see Freedman, "Family Planning in the Third World;" and Feeney, Griffith, et al., "Recent Fertility Dynamics in China: Results from the 1987 One Percent Population Survey," Population and Development Review, 15, 3 (June 1989), 297–322.
36. Glass, Population Policies and Movements in Europe, pp. 94–96.
37. Teitelbaum, Michael S., "Intersections: Immigration and Demographic Change and Their Impact on the United States," in World Population and U.S. Policy: The Choices Ahead, ed. Jane Menken (New York: W. W. Norton & Company, 1986), pp. 133–174.
38. Eckerson, Helen F., "Immigration and National Origins," The Annals of the American Academy of Political and Social Science, 367 (September 1966), 4–14.
39. Teitelbaum, "Immigration and Demographic Change," pp. 133–174.
40. Kennedy, Edward M., "The Immigration Act of 1965," Annals of the American Academy of Political and Social Science, 367 (September 1966), 137–149.
41. Teitelbaum, "Immigration and Demographic Change," pp. 133–174.
42. North, David, "Immigration Reform in Its First Year," paper no. 4 (Washington, DC: Center for Immigration Studies, November 1987).
43. Espenshade, Thomas J., "A Short History of U.S. Policy Toward Illegal Immigration," Population Today, 18, 2 (Washington, DC: Population Reference Bureau, February 1990), pp. 6–9.
44. Haub, Carl, "Immigration Reform Sweeps Congress," Population Today 18, 12 (Washington, DC: Population Reference Bureau, December 1990), p. 3.
45. Massey, Douglas, "Economic Development and International Migration," Population and Development Review, 14, 3 (September 1988), 383–413.
46. United Nations, Department of International Economic and Social Affairs, World Population Trends and Policies: 1987 Monitoring Report (New York: United Nations, 1988), pp. 235, 238, 259.
47. Ibid., pp. 219, 224.
48. Demeny, Paul, "Population and the Invisible Hand," Demography, 23, 4 (November 1986), 473.

49. Preston, Samuel, "The Social Sciences and the Population Problem," *Sociological Forum*, 2, 4 (Fall 1987), 619–644.
50. In his classic essay "The Tragedy of the Commons" (*Science*, 162 [December 13, 1968], 1243–1248), Garrett Hardin argues that individual needs cannot take priority over the common good.
51. Grigsby, Jill, "Democratic Constraints on Demographic Policy," *Comparative Social Research*, 7 (1984), 387–396.

SELECTED
REFERENCES

ENCYCLOPEDIAS

PETERSEN, WILLIAM, AND RENEE PETERSEN, *Dictionary of Demography: Terms, Concepts, and Institutions* (2 vols.), *Biographies* (2 vols.), *Multilingual Glossary* (1 vol.), (Westport, CT: Greenwood Press, 1985–1986).

ROSS, JOHN A., ED., *International Encyclopedia of Population* (New York: Free Press, 1982).

COLLECTION OF GENERAL POPULATION ARTICLES

FREEDMAN, RONALD, ED., *Population: The Vital Revolution* (New York: Doubleday, 1964).

MENARD, SCOTT, AND ELIZABETH MOEN, *Perspectives on Population: An Introduction to Concepts and Issues* (New York: Oxford, 1987).

PRESTON, SAMUEL H., ED., *World Population: Approaching the Year 2000.* Special edition of *The Annals of the American Academy of Political and Social Science*, July 1990, vol. 510.

SCIENTIFIC AMERICAN, *The Human Population* (San Francisco: Freeman, 1974).

TOMASSON, RICHARD F., ED., *Demography: Development, Dependency Theory, and Policy.* Special edition of *Comparative Social Research*, 1984, vol. 7.

WILLIAMS, ROBIN M., JR., ED., *Demography.* Special issue of *Sociological Forum*, Fall 1987, vol. 2, no. 4.

HISTORY OF POPULATION GROWTH

CIPOLLA, CARLO, *The Economic History of World Population* (Baltimore: Penguin, 1962).

CARR-SAUNDERS, A. M., *World Population: Past Growth and Present Trends*, 2nd ed. (London: Frank Cass, 1964).

COALE, ANSLEY, AND SUSAN COTTS WATKINS, EDS., *The Decline of Fertility in Europe* (Princeton, NJ: Princeton University Press, 1986).

GLASS, DAVID V., AND D. E. C. EVERSLEY, EDS., *Population in History* (Chicago: Aldine, 1965).

MALTHUS, THOMAS ROBERT, *Population: The First Essay* (Ann Arbor: Ann Arbor Paperbacks, 1959 [1798]).

MALTHUS, THOMAS ROBERT, ET AL., *Three Essays on Population* (New York: Mentor Books, 1960).

MCNEIL, WILLIAM H., *Plagues and Peoples* (New York: Anchor, 1976).

UNITED NATIONS, *The Determinants and Consequences of Population Trends* (New York: United Nations, 1973).

UNITED NATIONS, *World Population: Trends and Policies* (New York: United Nations, 1988).

UNITED NATIONS, *World Population Trends, Population and Development Interrelations and Population Policies: 1983 Monitoring Report*, vols. 1 and 2 (New York: United Nations, 1988).

UNITED NATIONS, *World Population Prospects 1988* (New York: United Nations, 1989).

U.S. BUREAU OF THE CENSUS, *Historical Statistics of the United States: Colonial Times to 1970, Bicentennial Edition* (Washington, DC: U.S. Government Printing Office, 1975).

WORLD BANK, *World Development Report 1984* (New York: Oxford, 1984).

WRIGLEY, E. A., *Population and History* (New York: McGraw-Hill, 1969).

POPULATION DISTRIBUTION

FREY, WILLIAM H., AND ALDEN SPEARE, JR., *Regional and Metropolitan Growth and Decline in the United States* (New York: Russell Sage, 1988).

PETERS, GARY L., AND ROBERT P. LARKIN, *Population Geography* (Dubuque, IA: Kendall/Hunt, 1983).

UNITED NATIONS, *The Prospects of World Urbanization* (New York: United Nations, 1989).

POPULATION AND ENVIRONMENT

BROWN, LESTER, ET AL., *State of the World* (New York: W. W. Norton and Company, 1990), and earlier editions.

EHRLICH, PAUL R., AND ANNE H. EHRLICH, *The Population Explosion* (New York: Simon and Schuster, 1990).

LAPPE, FRANCES MOORE, AND JOSEPH COLLINS, *Food First: Beyond the Myth of Scarcity* (Boston: Houghton Mifflin, 1977).

"Managing Planet Earth," *Scientific American*. Special issue, September 1989, vol. 261, no. 3.

WORLD RESOURCES INSTITUTE, WITH THE INTERNATIONAL INSTITUTE FOR ENVIRONMENT AND DEVELOPMENT AND THE U.N. ENVIRONMENT PROGRAMME, *World Resources 1988–89* (New York: Basic Books, 1989).

MORTALITY

HEER, DAVID, *After Nuclear Attack: A Demographic Inquiry* (New York: Praeger, 1965).

JOHANSSON, SHEILA, ED., *Aging and Dying: The Biological Foundations of Human Longevity* (Berkeley: University of California Press, 1990).

KITAGAWA, EVELYN M., AND PHILIP M. HAUSER, *Differential Mortality in the United States* (Cambridge, MA: Harvard University Press, 1973).

PRESTON, SAMUEL,   *Mortality Patterns in National Populations: with Special Reference to Recorded Causes of Death* (New York: Academic Press, 1976).
RUBENSTEIN, RICHARD,   *The Age of Triage* (Boston: Beacon, 1983).
UNITED NATIONS, DEPARTMENT OF INTERNATIONAL ECONOMIC AND SOCIAL AFFAIRS,   *Consequences of Mortality Trends and Differentials*. Population Studies, no. 95 (New York: United Nations, 1986).

FERTILITY

BEAN, FRANK D., AND GRAY SWICEGOOD,   *Mexican American Fertility Patterns* (Austin: University of Texas Press, 1985).
BLAKE, JUDITH,   *Family Size and Achievement* (Berkeley: University of California Press, 1989).
BULATAO, RUDOLFO A., AND RONALD D. LEE, EDS.,   *Determinants of Fertility in Developing Countries: A Summary of Knowledge*, vols. 1 and 2 (New York: Academic Press, 1983).
CALDWELL, JOHN,   *Theory of Fertility* (London: Academic Press, 1982).
CLELAND, JOHN, and JOHN HOBCRAFT, EDS.,   *Reproductive Change in Developing Countries: Insights from the World Fertility Survey* (London: Oxford University Press, 1985).
EASTERLIN, RICHARD, and EILEEN CRIMMINS,   *The Fertility Revolution: A Supply–Demand Analysis* (Chicago: University of Chicago Press, 1985).
FREEDMAN, RONALD, AND JOHN TAKESHITA,   *Family Planning in Taiwan* (Princeton, NJ: Princeton University Press, 1969).
HIMES, NORMAN E.,   *Medical History of Contraception* (New York: Gamut Press, 1963 [1936]).
LESTHAEGHE, RONALD, AND HILARY PAGE, EDS.,   *Child-Spacing in Tropical Africa* (London: Academic Press, 1981).
RINDFUSS, RONALD, S. PHILIP MORGAN, GRAY SWICEGOOD,   *First Births in America: Changes in the Timing of Parenthood* (Berkeley: University of California Press, 1988).
RINDFUSS, RONALD, AND JAMES A. SWEET,   *Postwar Fertility Trends and Differentials in the United States* (New York: Academic Press, 1977).
SACHDEV, PAUL, ED.,   *International Handbook on Abortion* (New York: Greenwood Press, 1988).
TEITELBAUM, MICHAEL S., AND JAY M. WINTER,   *The Fear of Population* (Orlando, FL: Academic Press, 1985).
WESTOFF, LESLIE ALDRIDGE, AND CHARLES F. WESTOFF,   *From Now to Zero* (Boston: Little, Brown, 1968).

MIGRATION

CLARK, WILLIAM A. V.,   *Human Migration* (Beverly Hills: Sage, 1986).
GREENWOOD, MICHAEL,   *Migration and Economic Growth in the United States* (New York: Academic Press, 1981).
HEER, DAVID,   *Undocumented Mexicans in the United States* (Cambridge, England: Cambridge University Press, 1990).
LONG, LARRY,   *Residential Mobility and Migration in the U.S.* (New York: Russell Sage, 1986).
MULLER, THOMAS, AND THOMAS J. ESPENSHADE, WITH DONALD MANSON, ET AL.,   *The Fourth Wave: California's Newest Immigrants* (Washington, DC: Urban Institute Press, 1985).
PORTES, ALEJANDRO, AND ROBERT BACH,   *Latin Journey: Cuban and Mexican Immigrants in the United States* (Berkeley: University of California Press, 1985).

AGE AND SEX STRUCTURE

EASTERLIN, RICHARD, *Birth and Fortune: The Impact of Numbers on Personal Welfare* (New York: Basic Books, 1980).

JONES, LANDON Y., *Great Expectations: America and the Baby Boom Generation* (New York: Ballantine, 1980).

LEE, RONALD D., W. BRIAN ARTHUR, AND GERRY RODGERS, EDS., *Economics of Changing Age Distributions in Developed Countries* (Oxford: Clarendon, 1988).

SEROW, WILLIAM J., DAVID F. SLY, AND J. MICHAEL WRIGLEY, *Population Aging in the United States* (New York: Greenwood Press, 1990).

POPULATION GROWTH AND ECONOMIC DEVELOPMENT

COALE, ANSLEY J., AND EDGAR M. HOOVER, *Population Growth and Economic Development in Low-Income Countries* (Princeton, NJ: Princeton University Press, 1958).

NATIONAL ACADEMY OF SCIENCES, *Population Growth and Economic Development: Policy Questions* (Washington, DC: National Academy Press, 1986).

SIMON, JULIAN, *The Ultimate Resource* (Princeton, NJ: Princeton University Press, 1981).

POPULATION GROWTH AND POLITICAL POWER

ALONSO, WILLIAM, AND PAUL STARR, EDS., *The Politics of Numbers* (New York: Russell Sage, 1987).

ORGANSKI, KATHERINE, AND A. F. K. ORGANSKI, *Population World Power* (New York: Alfred A. Knopf, 1961).

POPULATION POLICY

GLASS, DAVID V., *Population Policies and Movements* (Oxford: Clarendon Press, 1940).

LAPHAM, ROBERT J., AND G. B. SIMMONS, EDS., *Organizing for Effective Family Planning Programs* (Washington, DC: National Academy Press, 1987).

MENKEN, JANE A., ED., *World Population and U.S. Policy: The Choices Ahead* (New York: W. W. Norton and Company, 1986).

ROBERTS, GODFREY, *Population Policy: Contemporary Issues* (New York: Praeger, 1990).

WARWICK, DONALD P., *Bitter Pills: Population Policies and Their Implementation in Eight Developing Countries* (Cambridge England: Cambridge University Press, 1982).

COUNTRY STUDIES

BANISTER, JUDITH, *China's Changing Population* (Stanford, CA: Stanford University Press, 1987).

BOGUE, DONALD J., *The Population of the United States: Historical Trends and Future Projections* (New York: Free Press, 1985).

DAVIS, KINGSLEY, *The Population of India and Pakistan* (Princeton, NJ: Princeton University Press, 1951).

DYSON, TIM, AND NIGEL CROOK, EDS., *India's Demography: Essays on the Contemporary Population* (Atlantic Highlands, NJ: Humanities Press, 1984).

TAEUBER, IRENE B., *The Population of Japan* (Princeton, NJ: Princeton University Press, 1958).

DEMOGRAPHIC METHODS

PALMORE, JAMES, AND ROBERT GARDNER, *Measuring Mortality, Fertility, and Natural Increase: A Self-Teaching Guide to Elementary Measures* (Honolulu: East-West Center, 1983).
POLLARD, A. H., F. YUSUF, G. N. POLLARD, *Demographic Techniques*, 3rd ed. (Sydney, Australia, Pergamon, 1990).
SHRYOCK, HENRY S., JACOB S. SIEGAL, ET AL., *The Methods and Materials of Demography*. Condensed edition by Edward G. Stockwell (New York: Academic Press, 1976).

PERIODICALS

American Demographics, Demography, Family Planning Perspectives, International Migration Review, Population Bulletin of the United Nations, Population and Development Review, Population Index, Population Studies, Social Biology, Studies in Family Planning, U.N. Demographic Yearbook, World Bank World Development Report.
The Population Reference Bureau publishes *Population Bulletin* and *Population Today*.
The U.S. Bureau of the Census publishes *Current Population Reports, International Population Reports, and Statistical Abstract of the United States*

SOFTWARE

IMMERWAHR, GEORGE E., *Popshow* (Madison, WI: Wisc-Ware, University of Wisconsin Academic Computing Center). A collection of programs for teaching introductory demography or for self-instruction.
ISRAEL, BOB, DORIS SLESINGER, PETER UBOMBA-JASWA, AND KARL TAEUBER, *Population Pyramids* (Madison, WI: Wisc-Ware, University of Wisconsin Academic Computing Center). A two-part program that explains population age and sex structure and shows how to construct population pyramids.
KLAFF, VIVIAN, *UDemog* (Madison, WI: Wisc-Ware, University of Wisconsin Academic Computing Center). Computer assisted instruction for teaching demography.
MAXIS SOFTWARE, *SimCity* (Moraga, CA: Maxis Software). Simulates urban growth and the resulting social problems.
PSRC SOFTWARE, *Interactive Population Statistical System* (Bowling Green, OH: Bowling Green State University). Projects and simulates populations, illustrated with 2-D and 3-D graphs.
SELL, RALPH, *Future Population* (Raleigh, NC: National Collegiate Software Clearinghousse). Projects populations using cohort-component methodology.
SENDEK, ROBERT, *FIVFIV-SINSIN* (New York: The Population Council). Projects populations using cohort-component methodology.

INDEX